Michael Buckworth has written anyone considering setting up a b and learn from one of the best.

Duncan Cheatle – Co-founder of S
Learn Amp and The Supper Club (home to hundreds of the UK's most successful founders)

There are so many things founders have to get right in the first few months of their start-up's life, and the fear of getting something wrong can hold back even the most enthusiastic entrepreneur. *Built on Rock* explains what you should and shouldn't do, and is your best friend as you navigate the legal and business challenges of your new business. This is the book that will get ideas out of your head and turn them into a start-up.

Mirela Yordanova – Associate, LaunchLab Ventures

Michael Buckworth takes the reader on an educational journey from incorporation through launch and ending on raising an investment round. This is a must-read guide for students of entrepreneurship and anyone who wants to get a handle on the legal issues to think about when setting up a business.

Jerry Allen – Director for Entrepreneurship, UCL Innovation and Enterprise, Director of Enterprise Educators UK, Advisor to the UN

Built on Rock is written by one (legal) entrepreneur for another. However, forget legal speak, long words and complex explanations: this book focuses on what matters and gives practical advice on how to approach challenges. If you confuse your pre and post money, or think that fully diluted relates to the amount of ice in your G&T, this is a book you simply must buy.

Mark Tayler – Director, SFC Capital

Setting up a start-up can feel incredibly risky, particularly for young entrepreneurs. *Built on Rock* explains in simple terms how to identify and manage the legal and business risks inherent in a new business, without breaking the bank.

Jack Parsons – UK's Chief Youth Officer

Lawyers who can explain complex issues simply are few and far between: Michael Buckworth is one of them. *Built on Rock* brings Michael's in-depth knowledge of business and law, and over a decade of experience working with and helping entrepreneurs thrive in business. This is an essential guide for ambitious founders who want to set up in business, or take their existing start-up to the next level.

Chris Hancock – Founder of Crowd2Fund

Setting up a business is difficult with lots of pitfalls, but it's not rocket science. In this book, Michael demystifies the business and legal aspects by explaining in simple terms what founders should be most concerned about, and what they can sensibly decide to worry about later. This book is full of tips and advice drawn from Michael's work with many start-ups: every reader will discover something they didn't realise they didn't know.

Paul Grant – Founder of The Funding Game

BUILT ON ROCK

THE BUSY ENTREPRENEUR'S
LEGAL GUIDE TO START-UP SUCCESS

MICHAEL BUCKWORTH

First published in Great Britain by Practical Inspiration Publishing, 2021

Updated 2025

The moral rights of the author have been asserted

ISBN   9781788603072 (print)
           9781788603065 (epub)
           9781788603058 (mobi)

Every effort has been made to trace copyright holders and to obtain their permission for the use of copyright material. The publisher apologizes for any errors or omissions and would be grateful if notified of any corrections that should be incorporated in future reprints or editions of this book.

Practical Inspiration
Publishing

Contents

Building your start-up on rock

You're an entrepreneur. Maybe you always dreamed of setting up your own business, or possibly you were nudged in that direction by life's twists and turns. You might have been inspired to launch a new venture when you spotted a gap in the market, or been frustrated by something that didn't work and reckoned you could do better. Whatever your motivation, you have something in common with all other entrepreneurs: you feel a bit daunted by the scale of the task ahead of you.

Sure, it's a spine-tingling moment when a light-bulb goes off and you think, 'This idea could really happen!' That shiver of excitement, and the sneaking certainty that you're onto a winner, gets you revved up enough to take the first steps. But when you contemplate the myriad realities of creating a viable business, you may feel the energy draining away. There are so many things to work out. How can you make sure that no-one copies your work? Do you need employees, or would freelancers be better at first? What about insurance, contracts, and data protection? And that's before you've even contemplated what it takes to raise millions of pounds of investment.

It's right to think about these things, because if you don't take care about them, you'll be setting up your business for a host of problems down the line. Litigation, difficulties with gaining investment, and issues with employees and suppliers – these all come from a lack of understanding of the basics of start-up and investment law, some of which is unexpectedly complicated. It's where the old saying comes in: 'you don't know what you don't know'. This is the most dangerous gap in knowledge that you can have, because it creates a series of trapdoors that you can fall through where you least expect them.

It's also the reason that I've written this guide – to make the complex process of setting up a business and gaining investment straightforward. In these pages, I'll give you an understanding of the key legal and commercial issues that you should know about, and help you to find ways around the most common obstacles that stop entrepreneurs like you from succeeding with their businesses. In fact, this may be the book that your competitors will wish they'd read when they find themselves on the receiving end of a lawsuit, or when the juicy investment that they'd assumed was in the bag is cruelly snatched away because of the wrong paragraph in their shareholders' agreement.

None of this means that you have to become risk-averse or bogged down in detail. On the contrary, you'll be liberated. When your business is built on rock, you're free to fly as far or as high as you want, because you know that you have the basics right. You're not worrying about missing something crucial or landing yourself in expensive, hot water. Instead, you're able to take advantage of opportunities that might not have been available to you before, and have the time and energy to do what you're best at – coming up with new ideas, finding ways to make them a reality, and selling them to enthusiastic customers. Maybe even achieving world domination . . .

Why listen to me?

I'd like you to know that this book is written by one entrepreneur for another. I'm a different kind of entrepreneur to the ones that you may be used to, in that I'm a qualified solicitor. Ten years ago, I founded the only law firm in the UK working exclusively with start-ups and high-growth businesses, and I did it because I have a passion for entrepreneurialism. From product developers to cryptocurrency exchanges, from crowdfunding platforms to gaming start-ups, and from health-tech apps to video content producers, I've enjoyed supporting businesses in a wide range of sectors. Some have been incredibly successful. For instance, several have expanded into the US and Europe, selling their products to supermarkets around the world within five years of launch. Another client is currently signing deals left, right, and centre with banks and mobile phone providers eager for its ground-breaking security software. Without building their businesses on rock, these companies would never have been able to fulfil their potential, and it gives me pleasure to think that I've played a small but critical part in their success.

The idea behind this book is to share my expertise and experience so that you, too, can give your start-up solid foundations. Chapter by chapter, I walk you through a number of key milestones for your business, from creating a company to gaining investment – all from a legal and commercial perspective. Among other things, you'll discover:

- the irreversible mistake that some entrepreneurs make when they incorporate their companies;

- the painless way to limit what you'd have to pay out if a customer were to sue you;
- the simple step that will stop your suppliers, or even your co-founders, from ripping off your product;
- the one document that you should always get your solicitor to write for you, and why;
- the fundamental calculation error that will reduce the value of your business; and
- the little-known ways of attracting investors to invest in your company.

Because legal principles can be complex, I've done my best to make them simple. You won't find any dense, technical language here, only straightforward explanations and lively examples of other businesses that have succeeded and failed in their quest for growth.

To make things even easier, I've included two more elements. One is a start-up checklist, which you'll find at the end of the book. This is for you if you just want to know what your key tasks are and where in the book to find the detail, so feel free to head straight there if it suits you. The other is the story of Lucio, a fictional entrepreneur, whose story you can read as you go along. His ups and downs, and his struggles with some of his legal and commercial decisions, should reassure you that you're not alone – in fact, he's based on a composite of many of the founders I've worked with. I hope you enjoy his tale.

Finally, I should mention that the legal points in the second edition of this book are relevant for English law rather than that of other countries, and that any figures are correct for the tax year 2024/25. Many of the same principles apply wherever you are, but if you're not based in the UK you should ask for local advice.

Let's get started.

Meet Lucio

Lucio is our fictional entrepreneur, whose story I'm telling to make it easier for you to relate to the concepts in this book. This is a short introduction to his situation, and you'll find updates at the end of most chapters. It's up to you whether or not you read his tale – feel free to skip it if it's not your thing. But if you like a good story, read on.

★★★

The cafe window is starting to steam up but Lucio is enjoying watching the shoppers bustling back and forth, heads down and umbrellas high. It's a radical departure from his sunny home town in Italy, but he's in London now and loving every minute of it. The energy of the city hasn't lost its appeal, despite the rain.

Most of all there's work – lots of it. His marketing and business studies degree didn't get him far in Italy, and at first it didn't in the UK either. But after working in a couple of restaurants to improve his English, and gaining a proper job in a small online advertising agency, he's now working for a renowed boutique PR firm. Most of his clients are large, often global, technology businesses with offices in the UK.

At first he was expecting to spend his time on his clients' product marketing, but to his surprise their main requirement is for recruitment PR – they're desperate to hunt down the best and brightest people for their ever-expanding businesses. He's learning that the real problem these companies face is not only attracting applicants (although the free beer and rooftop gyms certainly help) but figuring out in advance whether the candidates have the right skills and experience for the jobs. Many of them turn out to be unsuitable or, if they perform well, end up leaving after a couple of years to work for a higher salary somewhere else. That makes training people after they've joined these businesses a costly risk.

Lucio turns away from the window and stares at the laptop in front of him. Taking a sip of his espresso (not exactly Milan standard, but you can't have everything) he ponders the business idea that he thinks solves this problem. It's an online, pre-recruitment skills platform that's tailored to employers, allowing them to upload bespoke training content that applicants are required to complete before they can apply for a job. The benefit to the employers is that they'll only have to interview pre-qualified candidates who have an adequate level of knowledge. The benefit to the applicants is that it opens a gateway to a job, as well as giving them new skills in the process. And the benefit to Lucio is that he can charge a fee to the companies for providing the software as a service.

Over time, he can see that there might even be the possibility of aggregating materials from different employers to allow them to deliver standardised training for specific sectors. There's also the potential for the system to grade the users, and give a recommendation to the companies they're wanting to apply to. This will lead to better-informed recruitment.

Although Lucio's feeling excited about making a profit from his new business, he also has major ambitions for it to have a social impact. He knows that not everyone has the benefit of a university education, and feels passionately about levelling the playing field for candidates who might be low on qualifications and experience, but high in talent. If his training platform could give skills to all applicants, and if employers could see who performed best, it would give some people a breakthrough opportunity. For this reason he wants to set it up as a social enterprise – one that will make a difference in the world.

By this point Lucio's fingers are flying across the keyboard as he outlines his business plan. He even has a name for his start-up: Pretrain.com.

As you read on in this book you'll follow more of Lucio's journey as he sets up his company, makes key strategic and financial decisions, and raises investment. The challenges he'll face are much the same as yours may be, so let's see how his journey goes.

PART ONE

Launching your business

Chapter 1

Setting up your company

Avoid the barriers and traps

You have an idea for your new business. You might even have tested it out, started exploring how you're going to fund it, and brought some co-founders on board to help you make it a success. It's an exciting time.

And yet it's also the moment at which you might feel a bit stuck. Do you set up a company, and if so what kind? Should you raise investment at the beginning, or wait until later on? Is it a good idea to plan out the finances up front, or to see how things evolve? And out of the myriad things you have to do, what should you focus on first? It can feel overwhelming.

I speak to lots of entrepreneurs who are at this stage, and what I find time and again is that it's easy to let the technicalities of setting up your business distract you from your main goal: to start creating your product or service and making money from it. I call them the 'Four Barriers'.

The Four Barriers

Barrier #1: worrying about what legal structure to use

Sometimes people spend months researching whether they should create a limited company, a social enterprise structure, or some other kind of entity. Please don't waste time on this. If you're in any doubt just set up a limited company, and you can always change it later – it's flexible.

Barrier #2: over-complicating the documentation

There's no need at this stage to over-engineer any legal documentation. In fact, if you think you need highly specialised legal or accounting advice before choosing your business structure, you're probably complicating things far too much.

Barrier #3: creating a complicated tax optimisation scheme

This is an eye-roller for solicitors and accountants (unless they're the kind who love to take your money, of course). As long as you're not setting up an investment fund or a business that will only work if it's highly tax-optimised, there's no need to even think about using an offshore structure.

The reasons for this are simple. Incorporating a company in a tax haven, such as the Cayman Islands, doesn't in itself mean that the company doesn't have to pay full UK tax. You also have to make sure that it's owned and managed from the

Caymans (generally by the use of a complex trust scheme). That costs a lot of money and is pointless for a start-up that, currently, has no value. What's more, UK investors won't be eligible for tax relief if they invest in your business, which is a huge disincentive for them. You can worry about offshoring your business later, when you have to spare the £50,000 that you'll need.

Barrier #4: getting bogged down in figures

Please don't spend ages creating fiendishly complicated cap tables, with varying predictions of the percentage holdings of shareholders or investors once you've been through five different investment rounds. At this stage you can spend your time more productively elsewhere. Excessive number crunching won't help you with the important tasks of setting up your company and making it a reality in the marketplace.

If any of these barriers are holding you back, you have full permission not to worry about them. Just push them to one side for now.

However, there are some elements of setting up a business that *are* worth thinking about from the beginning. If you don't get them right then they can make your life difficult, deny you future opportunities, and scupper your chances of securing crucial investment. So that you can avoid them, the rest of this chapter will cover:

- the vital differences between for-profit and social enterprise structures, and the impact these can have on your business' viability;

5

- what it means to create a company, and how to do it without causing future problems for yourself;
- how to pay yourself in a sustainable way; and
- the low-down on taxes and VAT.

For-profit company or social enterprise?

If your aim is to do good in the world, deciding whether your company should be a for-profit business or a social enterprise can be confusing. However, it's important that you understand the differences between the two set-ups if you're not to regret your choice further down the line. So that you can see what I mean, I'm going to explain what social enterprises are first and then move on to for-profit companies.

Social enterprises

Although you may hear the phrase 'social enterprise' bandied about, it's not really a legal term but a label that covers three broad types of business:

- Pure not-for-profit businesses. Here, all the money made is ploughed back into the business to pay its costs and expand its social purpose.
- Businesses that are created to support a social purpose or community, but still return some value to their owners and investors. You can often find these kinds of companies in the education space, for instance, where certain businesses have a core community purpose but still need to attract investment. This is

the kind of scheme that Lucio, our fictional entrepreneur, has in mind.

- Businesses that are primarily for-profit, but with the aim of trading in an ethical way or promoting a social purpose. Today an increasing number of start-ups are created with this aim, because entrepreneurs are often just as motivated by generating social change as they are by making money.

Does your business idea fall into one of these categories? If so, you may be thinking of setting it up as a formal social enterprise, but I'd probably advise you not to. To understand the reasons why, you need to know how these companies are structured and what that means for you. There are many different social enterprise structures, but here are the ones that crop up most often in the UK.

Community Interest Company (CIC)

This is the most common type, and is popular for businesses with a specific community purpose. It's usually set up in a similar way to a for-profit business (in that it has shareholders who own it), but with one crucial difference: it's subject to a statutory asset lock. This stops more than a certain amount of the profits (a maximum of 35 percent) being paid to shareholders.

It's worth thinking about the implications of this by comparing it to a standard for-profit company. In the latter, if you make £100,000 profit you can – in theory – pay out all of it to your shareholders. But with a CIC there's an asset lock, so you can't distribute more than £35,000. Discovering this limitation can be a major 'head in hands' moment for some CIC founders, and they often come to regret using this structure. How are they supposed to generate an income that both they and their shareholders can live on? What's more, once a business is structured via a CIC it's very hard to revert to a for-profit structure.

There is, however, one benefit to CICs, which is that social purpose grants are usually given only to asset-locked businesses. So if you think your funding will mainly come from grant money, a CIC makes absolute sense.

Company limited by guarantee

With guarantee companies, one or more people guarantee the liability of the company up to a certain amount. There are no shareholders or owners, and so no profits can be paid out. The only way to earn any money from such a company is to be a director or employee and be paid a salary. This structure tends to be used for charities and wholly not-for-profit entities.

You can see that a major sticking point with formal social enterprise structures is that there are restrictions on how they return value to their owners and investors. However, there's another disadvantage which is also of huge importance: these structures are not optimised to attract investment. The reason for this is a series of tax incentive schemes available to investors in start-ups. I'll explore them further in Chapter 10, but for now just be aware that the vast majority of UK angel investors use the schemes, and they're only applicable to for-profit businesses. There's an equivalent for social enterprises called social impact tax relief (SITR), but relatively few investors are interested in it. This means that being a formal social enterprise can close investment doors to you.

To me, the choice as to whether to use a formal social enterprise or for-profit structure largely comes down to how you expect to gain most of your funding. If it will be from community or social grants then you'll want to go down the social enterprise route, and if it will be from investors then you'll want the for-profit route. If you're not sure, a for-profit structure is simpler and more flexible (at least in the early stages) because you can run it pretty much how you like and – if it's important to you – still be socially responsible in the way that you do business. Also, while you can switch to being a social enterprise at a later date, *it's harder to do the same the other way around.* If your main aim is to trade ethically or to improve the world in some way, ask yourself whether you can achieve that better via a successful for-profit business.

For-profit businesses

So you've decided to set up a for-profit business. Your most likely structure will be that of a limited company, but it's worth understanding two other structures that are relevant: sole tradership and a Limited Liability Partnership (LLP).

Sole trader

When you set up in business as a sole trader, you're simply trading as yourself. All you need to do is to notify the tax authority, in the UK HMRC, that you're self-employed, and pay taxes on your profits at the end of the year.

However, the downside is that you're personally responsible for any losses that you make. So if your business goes bust, your home and assets are on the line and you can be made bankrupt. Just as importantly, if you have ambitions to build a sizeable business, being a sole trader isn't scalable. You can't raise investment, and it's more complicated to register for value added tax (VAT) and operate as a VAT registered business. We discuss VAT later in this chapter.

Limited Liability Partnership (LLP)

Some people set up LLPs because the owners have limited liability and the structure has certain tax advantages. Instead of the LLP paying tax on its overall profits, as happens with a company, the owners pay income tax on their individual shares of profits each year. However, LLPs are clunky to operate and not easy to scale. Also, investors prefer investing in limited companies because of the tax breaks available to people investing in those kinds of businesses. As a result, LLPs tend to be used only by professionals such as solicitors, accountants, and architects.

Limited company

This is the important one. A limited company is a separate legal 'person', owned by its shareholders. It can enter into contracts, borrow money, employ people, and sell shares in itself to raise money. It can do most of the things that people do, apart from make a mean cup of coffee and come up with cool ideas.

There are a number of advantages to setting up a limited company:

- it's the structure chosen by the UK government for investor tax reliefs, so investors are more inclined to invest in limited companies than they are in any other structure;
- the company has limited liability, so if its business goes bust the personal assets of its shareholders are protected;
- although the company pays tax on its profits (corporation tax), its shareholders don't pay any personal tax until they take money out of it, or sell their shares in it; and
- it's easy to set up and operate – in fact, ridiculously easy. In the UK you can do it yourself online, and there's no minimum sum you have to put in. This is in contrast to some other countries, where you have to invest the equivalent of thousands of pounds just to get a company up and running as well as jump through numerous bureaucratic hoops.

And the downside? It's more expensive to operate than if you're a sole trader. You have to file an annual corporation tax return and accounts with HMRC (which will probably cost you between £750 and £2,000 in accountancy fees), and lodge an annual confirmation statement with Companies House. Having said that, you can see how it's the structure you'd choose if you have aspirations for your start-up to be scalable and attractive to investors.

Setting up your company – what country to choose

If you're planning on incorporating your company in the UK you can skip this, but if you're thinking of basing it abroad there are some important things you need to know. You wouldn't want to deny yourself valuable opportunities, or saddle yourself with huge legal and accountancy costs for no reason.

Your number one consideration is where your investors are likely to be based, because investors usually prefer to buy into companies in the same jurisdiction as their own. This is when you might tell me you're planning on snaring some Silicon Valley cash and will therefore set up your company in the US, but you have to be realistic. If your initial customer base is in the UK or Europe, and if your main networks are also there, it makes little sense for you to set up a company thousands of miles away. Also, a UK company can attract UK investors who'll take advantage of the generous tax breaks from the government when investing in UK firms. If you incorporate abroad, you may be cutting yourself off from these.

So unless you have a really good reason to set up your company abroad, and have a clear plan as to how you're going to make it work, don't do it. Instead, think about where your networks are based, where you'll raise investment, and where your customers are located.

Setting up your company – what to do

Incorporating your business is one of those things that you'd think would be complicated and difficult, but isn't (unless you want it to be). Here's how to make it easy.

Set it up using Companies House

There are many providers who will happily incorporate your business for you for a fee, but you don't need them (or the endless cross-selling spam that you'll be bombarded with afterwards). Companies House is the best option, because it's the government's own system and also links your business into HMRC's corporation tax registration process. This saves you the hassle of working out how to do it for yourself. Just go to www.gov.uk/limited-company-formation/register-your-company.

Use standard articles of association

Articles of association set out the rules of your company, such as how you hold board meetings and appoint directors. When you register your company you'll be offered the choice of using standard articles or creating bespoke ones. The standard ones are fine. Please don't waste your time worrying about how to tweak the articles or getting a solicitor or accountant involved. You can always change them later if you need to, which will probably be when you carry out your first investment round or bring new shareholders on board.

13

Consider what address to use

You'll need a UK address at which to register your company. This is viewable on a public register, so you may prefer not to use your home. You can ask your solicitor or accountant for an alternative, which they'll often provide for a small fee. Whatever you do, bear in mind that important mail will be sent to this address, especially when your company is first set up. Make sure that whatever forwarding service you use is reliable.

Choose the right share capital

This is the only tricky part, but even so it doesn't have to be complicated. You just have to know what *not* to do.

Your shareholders are the owners of your company, so – at the risk of sounding simplistic – if it's made up of 100 shares and you own 50, you own half the company. When you incorporate, you're asked to pick a type of share. Choose 'ordinary' as these are the ones that allow you to vote, receive dividends (profits), and share in the proceeds when the company is sold. You can change this later if necessary.

You're then asked to pick how many shares you want your company to be made up of, and a nominal value for them. This is when it's easy to come unstuck. The nominal value has little relevance these days but it does represent a sum that you must pay into your company's bank account. Every so often I meet an entrepreneur who's got rather over-excited and decided to set up a company with 1 million shares at a nominal value of £1 each. Woohoo, that's a million-pound company right there! The problem is, as soon as they've clicked 'submit to file', they've committed to paying £1 million into their company's bank account.

If you were to do this, you'd have two problems. The first is that, on the off chance you don't have £1 million to hand, you now owe this sum to the company. You don't have to pay it – you can keep it as a loan – but HMRC will charge you interest on it each year (and on that kind of value, it adds up). Then, if the company were to go bust, the liquidator would ask you to stump up the cash to pay back the company. It sounds crazy, but it's the kind of mistake that takes five seconds to make and many months to undo. You either have to strike off the company and start again, or pay at least £5,000 to a barrister in a wig to go to the High Court and plead your case to reduce the share capital.

What should you do instead? I recommend incorporating with 10,000 shares at a nominal value of 1p each, which totals £100 of share capital. That's a sensible starting point and – as with much else – can be changed in the future if you want to.

Open a company bank account

You need an account in the name of the company, that's separate from your personal one. But who should it be with? Although the high street banks offer more comprehensive services than the challenger banks such as Starling and Tide, they have slow and somewhat archaic procedures for opening company bank accounts. If you want to speed up the process, or if you have foreign co-founders, you might want to go with a challenger. You can always switch to a high street bank later if you want to.

Appoint only one director at first, and make sure they're in the UK

There are two reasons for this. The first is that, when setting up a business account, the high street banks insist on at least one of your company's directors being resident in the UK. The second is that they carry out checks on every single shareholder and director, and require all of them to visit a branch with their IDs. As you can imagine, this is far easier if there's only one person involved. If you don't have any UK directors at all, I suggest opening an account with a challenger bank.

Once your account is opened you can appoint additional directors and issue shares to other shareholders. Most banks won't pick up on this for at least a year, by which time you'll have been able to sort out the necessary documentation. It's a doddle to add shareholders to a company after it's created – you just file a form SH01 with Companies House, and update your shareholder register.

As a side note, never include external investors in your shareholding at incorporation stage. It will void any tax relief they'd have been entitled to (more about this in Chapter 10).

Keep a look-out for your mail

When you set up a company, you find yourself opening a new brown envelope every week. They're mainly from Companies House and HMRC, and no matter how boring they look you should always keep them. The Companies House letter contains your online filing code, which you need for submitting your accounts and other documents online. The

HMRC letter has your company's Unique Taxpayer Reference (UTR), which you need when you register for VAT, file your accounts, and apply for tax reliefs. If you lose it, it can take months to receive a replacement.

You're not quite finished yet

You've set up your company and you've opened your bank account, so what's next to consider? You'll need to decide whether to register for VAT, how to pay yourself, and how to keep financial records.

VAT – to register or not?

VAT is a tax charged on most goods and services in the UK and Europe, at a default rate of 20 percent (there are other rates for certain types of goods and services). Whether to register for VAT is one of the most common start-up dilemmas for entrepreneurs. It may be that you have no choice but to register, as once your annual turnover hits the threshold of £90,000 it's compulsory. However, if you have the option, it's worth bearing in mind the pros and cons of registering early.

The advantage of being VAT registered is that you can re-claim the VAT you've paid in buying goods and services for your business, so that MacBook Pro you bought costs your company 20 percent less. The disadvantage is that you have to add VAT to what you sell, which, if your customers aren't VAT registered businesses who can re-claim it, makes you 20 percent more expensive. If you sell to consumers (in other words, the general public) try to delay registering for

VAT as long as you can, especially if you don't envisage any major VAT-able expenses. If you sell to businesses (who are mostly VAT registered and so can reclaim the VAT), however, it might make sense to register for VAT *before* you hit the threshold, so that you gain the benefit of reclaiming VAT on what you buy.

If you're registering early, my advice would be to ask your accountant to file the application rather than to do it yourself. HMRC is hyper vigilant about VAT fraud, and tends to ask early applicants a bunch of complicated questions which they can find difficult to answer. Far better to have someone who knows what they're doing to handle this than to let it become another barrier to getting your business off the ground.

And while we're on the subject of taxes, bear in mind that you'll be paying corporation tax on your company profits each year. You have to file a return twelve months after the end of your annual accounting period, but pay it nine months after the end of the same period. Bizarre, but true.

Paying yourself

I'm guessing that no matter how passionate you are about your start-up's mission, you'd quite like to earn some money from it. You can pay yourself through a salary as an employee of the company or, if you're a director, in dividends, or both. If you're paying yourself a salary your company will need to be signed up to PAYE, which is HMRC's online tax filing system for employee income tax and National Insurance contributions. Your accountant can sort this out for you.

If you want to be paid in dividends there are two points to consider. The first is that your company can only pay a dividend once it's profitable, which is why many entrepreneurs draw a salary instead at first. The second is that many company owners choose to pay themselves a salary up to the limit of the nil-rate tax band each month, which gives them the NI stamp but also means that they pay no tax. They then draw dividends for the rest of their income. Again, this is an area that's easy to change whenever you want to.

The downside of dividends is that they attract a tax bill at the end of the year. Many founders find themselves in trouble because they don't save enough money to cover their annual tax charge. At first, it might be worth paying a bit more tax on a monthly salary than be hit with a whopping great liability later on.

Keeping records

From day one, please get yourself some accounting software (there are plenty of options that are easy for non-accountants to use) and commit to entering your invoices and receipts on a weekly basis. This will ensure that you have accurate accounting records. Why? First, I've never understood how anyone can run a business without understanding its financial position. How else can you know what your profits are, how much to pay yourself, and what to charge your customers? And second, because you can save yourself a stack of money by presenting your accountant with a neat set of records when it comes to tax and VAT return time.

In the next chapter we'll look at the various risks associated with setting up a business, and how you can reduce them to give yourself the best chance of success.

The wrap-up

- Setting up a company is, for the most part, easy and straightforward. Don't let it be a complication that distracts you from the important work of developing your business.
- There are, however, some pitfalls that you should know about: setting up a social enterprise when you don't need one, basing your company abroad, and choosing the wrong share capital.
- When you're considering your finances, your VAT and tax liabilities are important aspects to take into account.

Lucio

When we last saw Lucio he was sitting in a London cafe, tapping at his keyboard as he mapped out his new business venture. Since then he's made some progress. He's consulted a couple of investors who've told him that, although his aim is to increase social mobility within the recruitment market, they're not prepared to back a social enterprise as they only invest in scalable for-profits. Given that it's going to cost him several hundred thousand pounds to create his online platform, and that there's no way he's going to gain it from grant funding, he's decided to go for a for-profit structure.

Lucio can immediately see that the sole trader route isn't an option even on a temporary basis because he won't be able to raise investment, so he sets up a company called Pre-Train Limited. He also registers it for VAT from the start, because his clients will be businesses. His ambition is to carry out his first major funding round in the US, so he initially plans to incorporate over there. However, after his conversations with investors, he sees that it wouldn't be a good idea as his network and initial target clients are in the UK and Europe.

Finally, he's also gained two co-founders. One is also in the UK (Peter, his CTO for technology development) and the other is in Germany (Sofia, his CMO for marketing and sales). Lucio is the primary shareholder and CEO, and doesn't issue shares to his co-founders just yet because he wants to make sure that he can open a bank account with no problem.

The basics are in place. Lucio has a limited company set up, he's VAT registered, he's opened a bank account, and he has two co-founders to help him drive the business forward. It's looking good, but there are many challenges still to come.

Chapter 2

Dodging the pitfalls

Identify and manage risk

It's raining as you stumble out of a bar at 1:00am. Pulling your coat over your head, you make your way to the train station but when you arrive you realise it's been closed for an hour. You need to find another way home, and you have a choice. You could call a taxi or you could flag down the nearest car and see if they'll give you a ride.

Let's weigh up the two options. The taxi is regulated (the driver has to be insured and vetted, and the car up to date with its MOT) so the risk of anything going wrong is small. Not so much with the passing car. You have no idea who the driver is and why they're giving you a lift, there's no record of you getting into their vehicle, and they may not even be insured. Even in your befuddled state you instinctively know that this option presents a greater risk.

We assess and manage risks all the time in our daily lives, and it's no different with our businesses. Taking risks is an inherent part of running a start-up, and if we're honest it's part of what makes it fun. You didn't become an entrepreneur because it was the safe option, did you? However, there's a difference between taking a calculated risk that's designed to bring you a benefit if it works out, and straying into dangerous territory unawares. Successful entrepreneurs make sure that they know what they're letting themselves in for in any scenario, and take steps to reduce their exposure to risk. Then they can spend their time and energy on the good stuff instead of dealing with problems that needn't have arisen in the first place.

Avoiding and managing risk is complicated by the fact that different risks apply to different types of business. If you're operating a restaurant, you might worry about giving food poisoning to your customers or people slipping on a wet floor and hurting themselves. If you're running a software business, you're more likely to worry about data breaches or a coding malfunction. It's a completely different picture in each case, but either situation could – in the most extreme situation – sink your business. It's that big a deal.

This chapter takes you through what kinds of risks your business could face and how you can minimise and manage them. We'll cover:

- legal risks;
- reputational risks;
- regulatory risks;
- financial risks;
- compliance risks; and
- trading risks.

You'll also learn how you can make strategic use of insurance to help you sleep soundly at night.

Legal risks

About three years ago, during the initial boom in legalised cannabis derivative products, a couple of co-founders approached my firm for help. They'd put together a detailed and realistic business plan for a venture to sell these products, and they had a crystal clear vision of what they were trying to achieve. It all looked good, but there was a teeny, tiny wrinkle in their proposal: they planned to plant vast fields of cannabis in rural Kent. This is the kind of activity that lands you in prison.

So the first question to ask yourself is: is my business idea legal? Being an optimist, I reckon that most people can figure this out for themselves, but as you've seen they don't always get it right. It's something to check out before you go any further.

Reputational risks

Some businesses are legal but still involve activities that aren't always socially acceptable. Escort services and certain types of pornography are good examples of this. There's nothing to stop you setting up this kind of business and promoting it, but you'll find that many web and mobile app platforms, and payment gateways, won't want to expose themselves to what they see as the reputational risks associated with your company. This can give you problems when you try to sell your products or services.

There are also certain types of business that are perceived (often unfairly) to be more attractive to criminals and fraudsters than most, such as those in the cryptocurrency space. Even if your only exposure to cryptocurrency is to allow payment in Bitcoin or Ethereum, the anonymised and non-centralised nature of these currencies means that there may be an increased risk of attracting the wrong type of customer. This can not only create problems for you, but may also mean that third party vendors and support services steer clear of you as well.

Regulatory risks

Just as you need to ask yourself whether your business is legal, you should also identify whether it operates in a regulated area. The main regulated sectors are financial services, medical products, services such as biotech and medtech, gambling, and the professions (law, accountancy, and architecture). If your business will operate within these, and if you'll be carrying out regulated activities, you may have to secure the appropriate clearances before you can start trading.

Financial services

Businesses in this sector are often subject to significant regulatory obligations imposed by the Financial Conduct Authority (FCA), including the need to be compliant with anti-money-laundering and terrorist financing laws. However, the good news is that many such businesses, particularly in the financial technology space, don't actually carry out regulated activities. Even if yours does, gaining authorisation is now much more straightforward than it used to be. What's more, you don't need to be directly authorised by the FCA but can 'rent' another company's regulatory clearance by becoming what's known as an 'authorised representative'. It's an expensive way of doing it but it's relatively quick and simple, allowing you to push out your product to market and start trialling it. If it works you can go for full authorisation later.

The FCA also helps start-ups through its regulatory sandbox, which allows you to test out an innovative proposition with real consumers but within the safe confines of its testing space. You can find further information at www.fca.org.uk/firms/innovation/regulatory-sandbox.

Medical services

If you operate in the medtech space you have two areas of risk to focus on. The first is patient safety, and the second centres on the processing of special category data (in your case, relating to health and illness). This is something we'll cover in a later chapter, but for now it's worth knowing that you have a serious obligation to get this right.

If you intend to sell your software to the NHS you'll need to comply with its guidelines and regulations. The NHS has a similar service to the FCA regulatory sandbox, allowing you to test your software with its application programming interfaces (APIs). This means you can check that you're meeting its standards, as a first step towards becoming a supplier. You can find it at https://digital.nhs.uk/developer/ guides-and-documentation/testing.

Financial risks

This is the big one. How do you intend to make money from your company? Have you thought it through? It sounds like such an obvious question that you may be tempted to stop reading, but please don't. It's surprising how deep the risks to your financial success can be if you make the wrong decisions at the wrong times. This is when it pays (literally) to think both long-term and strategically.

Lifestyle versus scalable businesses

In the start-up world there are two main types of business, which fulfil different needs for their owners. Understanding which kind you're setting up is vital if you're to make the right financial decisions:

- Lifestyle businesses: the aim of these is to provide an ongoing income, probably from the start, for their owners and investors.
- Scale-ups: the aim of these is to return value to their shareholders when they're sold, rather than through ongoing revenue.

Lifestyle businesses need to become profitable quickly so that they can pay their owners, investors, suppliers, creditors, and employees. If this is your type of business, your key financial questions are: how much money do I need to launch my business? And how quickly can I turn a profit? You'll want to be cautious about how much (if any) investment you seek and how much equity you give away in return – the more equity you give away, the smaller your share of profits.

Scale-ups tend to re-invest any profits in growth. Often (although not always) based online, they provide little or no income to owners and investors until they're sold – or at least until shareholders can sell some of their shares, probably to a venture capital (VC) in a later stage investment round. If your business is a scale-up, your key questions are: how can I pay my costs and expenses as they fall due and remain solvent until sale? How can I attract and retain enough users to give me the traction I need to sell at a high price? And how will I monetise those users? Unlike with a lifestyle business, you'll probably want to raise large amounts of investment throughout your company's lifetime. This will enable you to scale your business quickly and accelerate the time frame to exit.

Many tech businesses raise money at huge valuations without yet turning a profit, with Twitter being a classic example. In 2013 it listed for a valuation of over $14 billion even though it was significantly loss-making at the time. This approach to valuation would be unlikely to happen with a lifestyle business, because their valuations tend to be based on revenue or profit multiples. Twitter was able to list at this crazy valuation because it had such huge traction in its market. It's fair to say that the days of high-growth scale-ups being sold for vast amounts, despite having no proven way of monetising their users, are fading fast. Failure to think through monetisation can sink a scale-up. So often, I've seen clients raise a couple of investment rounds at really punchy valuations, only to find that they can't raise a further one because they haven't shown a coherent, deliverable route to making money. You need to figure out up front where your sales will come from, even if it may take time to get there.

In all of this, please don't forget your biggest financial risk of all: not managing your cash flow. Customers have a habit of paying late and it's easy to be unrealistic with your expenses, which can lead to you being unable to pay your debts as they fall due. Poor cash flow can kill a company in a frighteningly short space of time, no matter how amazing (and successful) the business idea behind it. However, it's an avoidable risk that you can manage by being on top of your book keeping. That way you'll always be aware of your costs and revenue, and who is and isn't paying on time.

Compliance risks

As an entrepreneur I don't imagine that rules are your favourite thing, but when you're in business there are certain ones that you have to follow. If you don't know about them, or don't have procedures for keeping to them, you expose yourself to the risk of being fined and – even worse – of having your brand name dragged through the mud.

Data protection and GDPR

This is a topic we'll cover later on, but just to flag up for now that it's a major compliance area that you'll need to plan for from the start. Lots of founders are scared of data protection compliance because some specialists try to make it seem as confusing as possible. However, the truth is that it's primarily about understanding the personal data you collect and putting in place processes to deal with it.

Payment Card Industry (PCI)

If you collect people's payment card data when selling to them you have to comply with onerous PCI standards. The easy way out of this is to use an established payment gateway that handles the problem for you. It will cost you more than taking payments yourself, but will seriously reduce your risk. These days it's rare for businesses to take and store card data themselves, as platforms such as Stripe are so accessible and widely adopted.

Chargebacks

This is especially relevant to you if you have a retail business. Chargebacks happen when a customer checks their credit card statement and sees a transaction that they don't recognise. They call their bank, who claws back the money from your business and refunds the customer. The banks do investigate these claims but they aren't always that thorough, despite the fact that some are the result of customer forgetfulness or fraud by a third party.

The risk for you is that you not only lose the money, but you also have to pay bank fees on top. Research shows that every £1 of chargeback costs the retailer £2.50. With chargeback rates in the UK being up to one percent of sales, this is a significant liability for your business which you'll need to include in your forecasting. There are ways to reduce chargebacks, such as ensuring that your trading name appears on your customers' statements, and notifying customers in advance of any payments that may come as a surprise.

Trading risks

You have to be an optimistic person to launch a business, and the assumption that nothing will go wrong is part of that mentality. Yet, as in all areas of life, bad things happen. We mess up an order. A customer is upset. We inadvertently cause a data breach. It's life.

However, the consequences of mistakes are far less dire if you have the right customer agreement in place. This vital document reduces your risks because it limits your liability and therefore protects your business. You can think of it as being like a bullet-proof vest. Hopefully you won't need it and sometimes it will seem a little cumbersome, but if the day comes that you're in the line of fire you'll thank your lucky stars that you took the trouble to put it on. We'll cover your customer contract in more detail in Chapter 5, but seeing as we're talking about risk at the moment it's worth understanding the most important reason for having this document: it limits your liability.

The word 'liability' means the state of being legally responsible for something, and you can exclude liability for most risks in your customer contract. Take, for example, a lead generation platform which has customers who use it to earn thousands of pounds a week in sales. A hurricane on the east coast of the US takes out its servers, crashing the site and temporarily removing a lucrative source of leads (this actually happened to one of our clients back in 2010). Without a standard clause that appears in most contracts, stating that the business isn't liable for lost profits, it could be liable for its customers' losses. This shows how including the right clauses in a well drafted customer contract protects your business.

Insurance – the risks and benefits

Putting in place the right insurance is one way of reducing the risks to your business. There are lots of different types of insurance, but I want to focus on the four most common.

Public liability insurance

This covers you for legal expenses and compensation claims if someone is injured at your premises, or if your business causes damage to someone else's property. Suppose you own a coffee shop and someone trips on a workman's cable snaking across the floor. The customer breaks their leg and sues you, and so your insurer pays up. This insurance is relatively standard and cheap.

Employers' liability insurance

At first you might not have any employees, but if you're aiming to grow that will soon change. Employers' liability insurance is mandatory if you have employees or workers, and provides cover in case any employee or worker is injured or becomes ill because they work for you. Classic examples are repetitive strain injury from keyboard work, or stress caused by the actions of you, your employees, or clients. You must have a minimum cover of £5 million, and again it tends to be fairly standard.

Professional indemnity insurance

This covers your business for claims arising from your negligence. For instance, if you own a software development company and one of your team mistakenly generates some code that allows users to access other people's personal data, you'll be covered if you're sued. Indemnity insurance isn't compulsory but given the huge risk of not having it, it's hard to come up with a good reason for not taking it out. The cost varies according to the type of business you operate.

Product liability insurance

This covers you in case any products manufactured and sold by you are defective. For example, if you sell a kettle that catches fire when left plugged in, this insurance would protect you. As with professional indemnity insurance, the cost varies depending on the products insured.

So those are the main types of insurance, but what factors should you consider?

The coverage

There are times when it could be advantageous to accept a level of liability in your customer agreement, even if the law allows you to entirely exclude it. This is especially true when you start taking on larger clients. If an investment bank, for instance, is paying you £10 million a year to licence your software, it's unlikely to tolerate a situation in which you're off the hook for any costs it incurs as a result of your code malfunctioning. So to gain the business you might agree to be on the hook for a certain amount of the bank's loss. You agree a cap on your liability to show that you have enough skin in the game and to convince your client you're serious about their business.

However, you must make sure that your insurance covers your potential (or 'contingent') liability. This is something that can catch you out, because when you first launch your business your clients might be small companies for whom you exclude all liability. However, as time goes by, your clients can become larger firms which require some skin in the game. Every time you sign a new contract in which you agree to any contingent liability, pull out your insurance policy and check that your coverage is sufficient.

Remember, though, that it's not only the total (aggregate) coverage you need to be sure about but the limit per claim. If your aggregate coverage is £10 million but your limit per claim is £1 million, you won't be covered if you've agreed with your client a capped liability of £5 million.

The cost versus the likelihood and impact of the risk

You might decide not to insure against a risk if it's extremely unlikely to happen, but what would be the exposure for you if it did? Would it cause your business to go under? Imagine you're importing £200,000 of goods from the Far East by cargo plane. Your insurance doesn't cover you for loss due to terrorism, which you might think is fine given that terrorists are far more likely to attack a passenger plane. However, if there were to be an attack, the size of the loss might cause your business to go bust. Do you insure or not? It's your call, but it's good to understand that the likelihood of the risk is not necessarily the same thing as the impact of the damage it would inflict.

The boring stuff

Given that I'm a solicitor, I have a high tolerance for reading boring documents. In fact, there's many an evening when you'll find me tucked up in bed reading shareholders' agreements while my better half huffs in disapproval. But even I hate reading insurance paperwork, because it's so boring and complicated (you might even think it's designed to be that way). And yet it's hugely important that you read at least the summary on the front page, because it contains everything you need to know about what is and isn't covered. You'd sometimes be surprised.

The excess

A couple of years ago one of our clients, an app development agency, asked an intern to research options for their professional indemnity insurance. The intern did a great job of reducing the renewal premium, and everyone was happy. Later that year, one of the developers made a hideous mistake with their coding and a customer sued the company for millions of pounds. That wasn't great, but they were insured. Except that when they went to claim, the excess turned out to be £100,000 (so *that* was how the intern had reduced the price). The firm couldn't afford the excess and went bust. The lesson? If you can't afford to pay the excess, you're not insured.

The exclusions

Logic doesn't always apply here. When I read the summary of a renewal quote for our office insurance recently, I was amazed to discover that neither our buildings nor our computer equipment would be covered for fire and theft. What was the point of the insurance? I took our business elsewhere.

If you're finding all this talk of risk a bit overwhelming, I've created a risk grid that you can download for free. This will help you to think through the specific risks associated with your business. Just go to www.buckworths.com/riskgrid

The point of solicitors

The joke is: how many solicitors does it take to change a light bulb? As many as you can afford.

Wisecracking aside, the point of solicitors is to help you to identify and reduce the risks in your business. When you buy a house it's likely to be your most significant investment, so you don't think twice about appointing a solicitor to make sure that it's not about to be knocked down to build a motorway, for example. Why, then, wouldn't you use a solicitor to help you protect the business that you're going to spend most of your time on and that will, hopefully, end up being your most valuable asset?

A common misconception is that the job of solicitors is to draw up documents. Of course, documents are what often comes out at the end of the process, but they're not the main purpose. They're the end result of a detailed analysis of your business risks, and they protect you from being sued. Your documentation is an investment in your company's security.

You may have found template legal documents online for a fraction of the price of what you'd pay a solicitor. They seem okay, so why not use them? Because they're generic and not specific to your business. They're sold by companies that may look like law firms, but are actually neatly-marketed sales platforms. The people who run them aren't insured or regulated as solicitors, nor do they provide detailed, tailored advice. Your specific business risks depend on the sector your company operates in, what kinds of customers you want to attract, the level (and timing) of any investment you need, and your aims as an entrepreneur. These are crucial variables, and there are many more. No generic set of terms and conditions can hope to cater for them all in a way that will protect your business from going under if the worst happens. That's the difference between paying £20 for a template document and, say, £4,000 for one drawn up by someone who's experienced, regulated, and insured. It's also the difference between your business being built on sand, and being built on rock.

As a final note, anyone can call themselves a 'lawyer' and provide legal documentation such as terms and conditions. Solicitors, however, are bona fide legal professionals. It's a good idea to check the Law Society website to make sure that you're dealing with a qualified solicitor. It's at https://solicitors.lawsociety.org.uk.

In the next chapter we'll explore the benefits of protecting your company's intellectual property, and how to go about it.

The wrap-up

- Ignoring risks, or not being aware of them, can potentially sink your business.
- Legal, reputational, regulatory, financial, and compliance risks can all be managed – as can pretty much any other type of risk.
- A qualified solicitor is the best person to help you with this process.
- Having the right insurance is a key way of reducing your risks.

How's Lucio doing?

Now that Lucio has set up his company, he's getting excited about raising investment. However, he remembers his uncle Stefano, who lost all his money in a start-up that was sued by its main client for a mistake by one of his employees. That's the last thing that Lucio wants to happen to Pre-Train.

So how can he guard against things going wrong? It strikes him that it would be a good idea to speak to his uncle to see what he can learn. Stefano, now older and wiser, tells him that the first thing Lucio should do is to speak with a solicitor about risk. This isn't what Lucio had in mind, but to keep Stefano happy he makes an appointment with a commercial solicitor to talk things through. He comes out of the meeting extremely glad that he did.

He learns that his first concern should be reputational risk, because his software will allow third parties to publish their own content on his platform. The solicitor tells him that his customer contract should give him the ability to ban, and if necessary take down, illegal content or material that infringes someone else's intellectual property. Another focus should be financial risks. His platform will be a scale-up, requiring significant investment up front to set up and operate. He discovers that he won't earn anything from it for a while, so he needs to plan his personal finances around that.

The final two areas relevant to Lucio are compliance and trading risks. Pre-Train will gather data about its users, and also host bespoke training documents belonging to its corporate customers, so he'll need to ensure data security. He also thinks about what could go wrong when he starts trading. The platform could crash, training materials could be accessed by the wrong people, confidentiality could be breached, or a company could hold him responsible if they end up hiring someone who doesn't work out. Lucio concludes that he'll need various disclaimers in his customer agreement that exclude liability for these areas.

As for insurance, he only needs professional indemnity for now. He'll look at public and employer's liability insurance when he has an office and employees to consider.

Chapter 3

Protecting your brand and intellectual property

Secure your intangible assets

Now you have a business idea and have set up a company, you'll be turning your thoughts to your product or service and how you're going to brand it. Until you have something to sell, and a compelling way of presenting it, you don't have a business.

What makes a brand? It's a mixture of elements: your product name, logo, website design and content, social media images and videos, and any other visual or written work (called 'intangible assets') that you come up with. Together with your product or service, these are uniquely yours, and you wouldn't want anyone else to copy them and pass them off as their own. They make up a significant part of the value in your business, so you need to make sure that they're properly protected.

This is where the notion of 'intellectual property' (IP) comes in. When your business owns the IP in its various intangible assets, it's as if you've set up a special force shield around them as protection. The good news is that you don't need to be a Jedi warrior to do this, you just need to know how to claim ownership of your IP. In this chapter I'll cover what forms of IP you need to be aware of, how to protect them, and ways of ensuring that you don't get into trouble by encroaching on someone else's.

Your business idea: why it's precious (and why not to be precious about it)

An idea can't be protected, but its execution can be. Suppose that one day, while grappling with the wires trailing from the back of your TV, you have a brainwave about creating a special attachment that slips into it to hold an extension lead. You mention this to your friend. If that 'friend' were to steal your idea and set up a business making a similar attachment, there's not much that you can do to stop him. However, if you've already created the product before you show it to him and it's only then that he copies it, you may be able to prevent him from manufacturing it because it would infringe your IP rights.

The unfortunate outcome of this is that some entrepreneurs are terrified about sharing their ideas before they're executed, because they worry that someone will swipe them from under their noses. Of course, this can happen and there are some high-profile examples out there to scare you, such as that of the Winklevoss brothers who famously claimed that Mark Zuckerberg stole their ConnectU idea to create Facebook (something he denied). However, in my experience the risk is small, and I firmly believe that the first step towards creating a successful business is to gain early feedback on your idea from as many people as possible. To do this, you need to talk about it. So many of the good things that have happened to me as an entrepreneur have been the result of me telling people about what I do.

You'll probably start with your partner, your family, and some of your friends, and their reactions will tell you something useful. However, they likely have similar backgrounds and life experiences to you, so their opinions may just reinforce your perspective. They'll also be tempted to tell you what you want to hear, rather than what you need to know. It's people outside of your network who have the most useful input to give, and they may also be prepared to challenge you more. This will help you to test your idea and improve it.

But what if they steal it? This is where it helps to take a step back. You're an entrepreneur, and naturally you're convinced that your idea is a game changer. If you weren't, why would you be throwing your life into pursuing it? And yet other people are more interested in their own ideas than they are in yours – they don't want to spend time, money, and energy on something they didn't come up with themselves. This is especially the case if they're a potential investor. Investors work with a simple model: give you money so that you slug your guts out for the next five years to make them rich. They're investing in you and your idea, not in doing the heavy lifting.

Every week I speak with 15 or 20 entrepreneurs, each of whom explains to me their business idea. With the contacts I've built up over the years it wouldn't be difficult for me to pull together a team to replicate any one of them, but why would I? I have my own business to run. What's more, behind their idea (and invisible to me) is a detailed plan of what they want to achieve, why they think it will work, and a life journey that has led them to this moment. That isn't something I could copy, even if I wanted to.

In fact, *not* talking about your idea is the one thing that guarantees that your business will fail. If you live in a bubble and don't gain any feedback at all, you'll almost certainly find that your product will come out slightly 'off whack' because it's based purely on what you've imagined in your head. The most successful business ideas are adapted as a result of what people say about them, so please seek as much feedback as possible before you launch.

Who owns your IP?

Ideas are important but so is owning what you create. Every person who contributes to your business is the potential creator of valuable pieces of IP: products, designs, written copy, source code, images, and other assets. However, if that person isn't an employee (in other words, someone who's classified as being employed by your business and is paid through PAYE), the IP belongs to them and *not to you or your company*. Even if you paid them for the work.

For instance, if you ask your graphic designer friend Katy to design your logo, and you give her £50 plus a bottle of wine as a thank you, that logo belongs to her. At best there's an implied licence that you can use it, but she could withdraw it at any time or demand a fee for its continued use. You might think she'd never do that because you've known her for years, but consider how many other friendships in your life have come and gone. People drift apart, have fallings-out, or just move onto other things. You can't risk someone else owning IP that's needed by your business.

So what should you do to avoid any problems? You ask Katy to sign an IP transfer agreement, which can be done in one of two ways. The first is as a clause in her customer contract with you, stating that any IP generated by her for you belongs to you, either from the point of creation or once you've paid for her services. Never accept a clause in such a contract that says the ownership of the IP remains with her, even if there's a licence for you to use it. If her business were to go bust the licence could terminate, meaning that you'd no longer have the right to use the logo. The second way applies if you don't have a contract with Katy, in which case you'll need a standalone IP transfer agreement. This is a standard two-page document that transfers the IP of what she's created to your business, and is simple and quick to do.

The people who create IP for your company aren't limited to contractors, freelancers, and other suppliers, but can be co-founders as well. In fact, the most common IP issues tend to arise between co-founders and the story is always the same. They set up a business together, perhaps to create an app. At that stage they're excited, everything is fantastic, and they're all going to be millionaires. They want to get going and start making money so they don't bother with IP transfer agreements. However, some time later the CTO, whose coding was fundamental to the creation of the first version of the software, becomes less pivotal to the business. He feels sidelined, falls out with his co-founders, and walks. The problem is that he owns the IP in the source code of the company's app, which gives him a massive bargaining chip that he can use to extract money from the business. He can even withdraw the company's right to use the code, which would be disastrous.

My message is clear: ask everyone who creates IP (including your co-founders) to sign a simple IP transfer agreement up front. This transfers everyone's IP to the company so that it becomes a business, rather than a personal, asset.

Checking for competing IP

The point of IP is that it belongs to a person or company, and therefore can't be used by anyone else. But what if you're just starting up your business and haven't created any assets yet? You need to make sure that what you intend to do doesn't infringe on anyone else's IP and cause you problems down the line. However much you love what you've come up with, it makes no sense to pour your energy into it only to find out six months later that someone else got there first.

So, before you create your product name and branding, please carry out some basic searches to see what your competitors are already doing. It astonishes me how often entrepreneurs tell me that they have a fantastic brand or idea that's completely unique. And yet I only need to do a quick Google search to find that six other businesses are doing the same thing, or using the same or a similar brand.

Here are the checks that you can do:

Domain names

You don't want to create a brand that has no domain name available for it. I suggest that you type your brand name into one of the domain name provider sites, such as 123Reg or

GoDaddy, and they'll show you what is and isn't available. If you're okay to go ahead it makes sense to buy all the domains you may need, with different domain endings and spelling variations, so that no-one else can use them. If the domain isn't available, enter it into your browser to see if it's a competitor who holds it.

Social media profiles

Check for variants of your brand name on Instagram, Facebook, Twitter, YouTube, TikTok, and any other relevant platforms. Not only will this tell you if you'll have problems setting up an account under your brand name, but it will also indicate if anyone else is using your brand already.

Trademarks

Run a simple trademark search using the Intellectual Property Office's (IPO) search tool at www.gov.uk/search-for-trademark. If lots of similar marks come up, or if you can't work out whether they would cause you a problem or not, ask a solicitor to help you. They can also search on foreign databases to see if there are competing marks in your target markets (I'll cover trademarks in more detail in a moment).

Google search

It sounds obvious, but just enter your brand name into a search engine and see what comes up. Sometimes the most obvious course of action is the most overlooked.

Different types of IP

There are four main types of IP to focus on when setting up your business. They are:

- copyright;
- design rights;
- trademarks; and
- patents.

I'll go through each of these so you can see how they relate to your product or service.

Copyright

This protects an original, creative work and stops others from using it without the owner's permission. It's the most common form of IP because it relates to most of the intangible assets of your business, such as the content of websites, marketing materials, logos, videos, written content, images, and – importantly – source code. Many people think that they need to register the copyright in a work to own it, but in the UK it arises automatically as soon as it's created. If you want a record of the date of creation, you can email it to your solicitor or accountant so there's a timestamped record. Also, although you don't need to, you can mark your content with the copyright symbol ©, your company's name, and the year of creation. This flags up that it's subject to copyright.

In addition to ownership rights, a copyright creator also has 'moral rights'. These include the right to be identified as the author of the work, object to how it's presented, and also to changes being made to it. This means that even if you own the copyright, you can't do much with it if the creator of the material retains the moral rights. For instance, if Katy the designer was happy to transfer the IP for your logo but didn't also waive her moral rights, she could prevent you from changing the colour or tweaking the font. So your IP transfer document should also include a waiver of moral rights, which isn't something that service providers always offer in their terms of service.

Design rights

These are rights that aren't widely known about, but can make a significant difference when it comes to protecting your product or brand from being copied. Under UK law, the creator of a design automatically holds the design right for ten years after it was first sold (or fifteen years after it was created, whichever is the earliest). This enables the creator to stop someone else from copying their design.

What kinds of designs do these rights cover? They apply automatically to the shape and configuration (how the different parts of a design are arranged together) of all three-dimensional objects. So if you design a tool for opening sticky jar lids, for instance, you hold the design rights for it without having to do anything – assuming you have the right IP agreements in place, of course.

You can also claim ownership of the design rights for two-dimensional items, such as graphics and textiles. The difference is that you have to register your rights to guarantee protection for them, although this is a relatively cheap and simple process. All you have to do is apply through the IPO by filling in a form, which costs £50 per design.

This is an extremely worthwhile way of protecting your logo, website design, and other intangible assets – I've even seen it done for restaurant menus. Any design that's integral to your brand, and that you wouldn't want people to copy, can be protected in this way. In fact, you can have a logo or any other design protected as a design right as well as, or instead of, a trademark. Sometimes it's a better way of protecting the graphical representation of a logo than a trademark (and considerably cheaper), as you'll see in the following section.

Trademarks

The purpose of owning a trademark is to give you a monopoly on the use of your brand name, logo, or marketing strapline in the course of trade. However, this only relates to the country and classifications of goods and services that you've registered the trademark in. For instance, my firm holds the UK trademark for the term 'StartupRoar', which is used for publishing online content for start-ups. The trademark covers two classes of services: legal services and publishing. If someone were to launch a blog for entrepreneurs in the UK and call it 'StartupRoar', we could stop them as they'd be infringing our trademark in the same goods and services. But if it was a football team for start-up founders, our hands would be tied.

Filing a trademark in the UK is deceptively simple – you just have to fill in a form via the IPO's website at https://trademarks.ipo.gov.uk/ipo-apply. It doesn't even cost much:

£270 for a UK-only trademark covering three classes. However, trademark law is fiendishly complex and there are many pitfalls for the unwary. I strongly suggest that you use a solicitor to file your application rather than doing it yourself, due to the following potential outcomes.

First, if your application happens to infringe on the rights of an existing mark holder they can ask to have your application struck out. You may also receive an aggressive letter from their solicitor telling you to back off, which might make you panic and change your brand. However, if you use a solicitor yourself you probably won't have the problem in the first place, because they'll carry out thorough-enough searches to pre-empt it and may be able to draft around any issue. Even if you do, you can leave the unpleasant hassle to them.

Second, your application could be refused because it doesn't meet the requirements for a trademark, such as because it lacks distinctiveness. Now you've not only wasted your money but, more importantly, you've created a record of the refusal, which makes it difficult if you want to re-apply later.

Third – and this is the worst potential outcome – your trademark could be approved. Joyfully you spend a huge amount of money on creating and promoting your brand. Then a couple of years down the line, once everyone knows who you are, you receive an objection from a competitor or other third party. That's okay, you think, you registered the trademark ages ago. But wait. Just because the IPO approved it, doesn't mean that it's necessarily enforceable or can't be challenged by anyone else – all it means is that it's gone through the IPO's standard process. If you're not prepared to re-brand, your competitor could take you to a tribunal, the outcome of which might be that they'll win, or even that the judge will decide your mark is invalid for some other reason and strike it out. Now you're left high and dry.

It all comes down to managing risk. Your brand is hugely important to your business and you're going to spend a lot of money on promoting it. Why wouldn't you want to make sure that it's safe to use right from the start? What's more, legal fees for trademark applications aren't particularly expensive. A standard UK one, including searches and dealing with the regulator, will probably cost you around £1,000 compared to £270 for doing it yourself.

The situation grows in complexity if you're wanting to register a mark in more than one country. There's a way of doing this through the World Intellectual Property Office, which allows you to select all the countries you want by paying a fee starting at 653 Swiss Francs. 'Great!' you think. However, once you've filed your application you'll be bombarded by communications from each country's individual regulator asking you to pay a filing fee and provide an application in an official language of their country. Someone (who must have a lot more time on their hands than me) has calculated that the filing fees for all the relevant countries would come to around £25,000, with translation costs of £35,000. It's far better to pick the individual countries in which you intend to trade, and focus on those to start with.

Reading all this might lead you to believe that applying for a trademark should be one of your top priorities, but I don't think the application itself is the most important task on your list. Running the searches, and checking that your brand is 'clean' and won't infringe on anyone else's existing trademarks, is far more vital.

Patents

You can use a patent to protect certain types of invention because it gives you the right to take legal action against anyone who makes, uses, sells, or imports it without your permission. To be granted one your invention must be all of the following:

- something that can be made or used;
- new; and
- inventive (not just a simple modification to something that already exists).

Only certain types of invention can be patented, but if yours can, should you go ahead? It depends. Patent applications are fiendishly complicated so you need a specialist advisor, and the whole process will probably cost upwards of £50,000. Patents do play a crucial role in certain types of businesses, such as ones that create something that's genuinely innovative like a pharmaceutical drug, specific tool, or machinery. But for many start-ups, such as professional services or software providers, I think they're of little value. A far better use of your £50,000 is on marketing your products and developing traction with your customer base – spending it on a patent can actually damage your business when you look at it that way.

There's another reason why obtaining a patent can be harmful: it can only be secured if your invention is not yet in the public domain. But how do you gain vital feedback on your idea if you can't talk about it? You can see how going down the patent route could inhibit your ability to do market research and also delay your launch, which is why the time and energy you spend on it may be better spent on launching your business. Most companies create success through traction and reputation, not through owning patents.

In the next chapter we'll dive into the pros and cons of employing people, and how you can incentivise them through shares and options.

The wrap-up

- IP arises in the execution of a business idea, not in the idea itself – that needs exposure and feedback.
- Make sure that your company, rather than the people who contribute to it, owns all of its IP.
- Check for competing IP before you make any big decisions on branding.
- Copyright, design rights, trademarks, and patents are all ways of protecting your business – but you don't need them all.

How's Lucio doing?

Now that Lucio has analysed the risks for his business, he turns his attention to protecting his IP. His first assumption is that his software will incorporate a clever algorithm that he thinks would be patentable, and it seems like a good idea to protect it. So he talks to a patent attorney. This teaches him that, while it might be possible to gain a patent, it wouldn't be a good use of his limited funds. The most important thing is for him to get feedback on his idea, launch his platform so that people can start using it, and gain some traction.

He also runs a trademark search for Pre-Train. The search comes up clear with no exact matches, but there are some similar brands in Lucio's classes of goods and services, such as Pro-Train. Luckily most of them are in the health and fitness industry rather than in his field of recruitment and training, but he decides to make an early application just in case there's any opposition. He asks a solicitor to help him so it's done properly.

Lucio is starting to formalise all aspects of his start-up now, and investing in protecting his IP adds to his feeling that it's really happening. He's fully committed to making his idea a successful reality.

Chapter 4

Bringing in help

Incentivise employees and contractors

If you're going to run a successful company you can't do it on your own – you need help. But what form should that help take? There are a number of options, and your choice should be based on the skills and talents that you need to complement your own as the business owner. They include:

- bringing in a co-founder with responsibility for a specific area of your business;
- outsourcing a function entirely (this can be a good way of buying in legal and accounting advice);
- retaining a contractor (someone who doesn't work for you, but who may spend time in your office and be semi-integrated with your permanent team);
- recruiting experienced, independent advisers to help with areas such as setting strategy and raising investment; and
- employing people directly.

There are no concrete rights or wrongs to how you bring on board knowledge and talent. The most important thing is that you think carefully about what would work best for your business, and how you ensure that you receive value for it. That's what we'll explore in this chapter.

Getting the balance right

I tend to find that there are two extremes when it comes to entrepreneurs managing their teams. The first is the person who's determined to understand every last detail of what everyone is doing, which can waste an astonishing amount of time. This founder finds it hard to delegate and doesn't realise that their own core skills are what's most important to focus on. The second is the person who's fascinated by their own area of expertise and has no interest whatsoever in anything else. This is a luxury they can't afford, because they need to have enough of an involvement in all aspects of their business to know what's going on – at least at a top-line level.

It's not an easy balance to get right. Launching a start-up involves embarking on a steep learning curve – you have to gain a basic understanding of accounting, marketing, law, and a whole bunch of other specifics. However, that doesn't mean that you should become an expert in each area. The personal value you bring is a mixture of your core expertise, your passion, and your business acumen – so focus on these. Embrace your strengths and be aware of the skills you lack, because you can always buy them in.

One of our most successful clients has used his sharp business instincts to grow a company which now has a multi-million-pound turnover. He can negotiate, spot a good deal, and imagine how to market a product. What he doesn't understand are cap tables, the impact on his business value of giving away shares, or the implications of agreeing to various investor terms. That's fine, because he focuses his energy on what he's good at and uses solicitors and accountants to manage, figure out, and explain to him what he finds difficult.

If you're looking for an area of your business to get to grips with that's outside of your expertise, I suggest that you start with your accounting. Every entrepreneur should buy a licence for an online accounting software package, and personally input the company's expenses and income on a weekly basis for the first few months. It's the single best way of understanding the financial drivers of your business. Think of the hapless founders on 'Dragons' Den' who stammer and sweat when asked how much it costs to manufacture one of their products. They should be able to rattle off the numbers without thinking. How else can they decide how to price it, what their marketing budget should be, and where to sell it? After a while you can stop being so hands-on with the book keeping and outsource it, just not at first.

Employee or contractor?

One of the key issues that you might be grappling with is whether to employ people or hire them as contractors or advisers. To decide on this you need to be clear about the mechanisms for tax and National Insurance (NI), the varying legal obligations on you as a business owner, and the different ways that potential investors see employees as opposed to contractors.

Tax and NI

Employees: these are people whose pay you record via HMRC's Pay as You Earn (PAYE) system. You have to deduct their income tax and employee NI at source and pay it to HMRC, as well as pay employer NI contributions.

Contractors and advisers: these are people whom you pay when they invoice your company. You pay them in full without deducting any tax or NI, as it's the contractor who's responsible for paying that at the end of the financial year. Also, you don't pay employer NI contributions for them.

You can see that there's a significant difference in tax treatments between employees and contractors, with HMRC gaining immediate and regular payments from employees but having to wait longer (and for less) from contractors. This is the main reason why HMRC is always keen to reclassify contractors as employees when it can, and it does this through legislation that defines what an employee is. There are a number of criteria, but the main ones relate to control and risk. The greater the control you have over how and when someone does their job, the more likely they are to be an employee. The greater the risk that they take (for instance, investing in their own equipment and training), the more likely they are to be a contractor.

It can be tempting to keep costs down by hiring everyone as contractors. However, if you bring in a contractor and six months later HMRC decides that the true nature of their relationship to your business is that of an employee, the consequences can be severe. HMRC might force you to pay all the tax and NI contributions that you should have deducted from their wages, as well as the employer NI contributions, plus interest and penalties. This is in addition to what you've already paid the contractor for their services. So a 13.8 percent saving on employer NI contributions can end up costing you another 50 percent of your contractor's salary. Make sure that you understand the risk you're taking before going down this path.

Personally, I don't see the need to treat people as contractors when they're really employees, because the downsides of employing people are minimal nowadays. Some business owners worry about the commitments they have to employees, but within the first two years you can usually ask them to leave without giving a reason so you're unlikely to be stuck with someone who doesn't perform. As for insurance, health and safety, and HR issues, if you have physical premises you already have to comply with health and safety legislation for anyone who comes into your building. You also have to have employers' liability insurance for contractors who are based in your office, and data protection and IT policies in place for both types of workers. So, in terms of your obligations, there's not as great a difference between an employee and a contractor as you might think.

To be fair, there are additional financial responsibilities you have to employees such as holiday and sick pay and pension contributions. But statutory sick pay isn't much, and pension payments are only a small element of salaries. Plus, you have the benefit of an employee's full commitment to your business. They'll grow with it and help to develop it, and are far more loyal than contractors. As a firm, we always put people on payroll regardless of their relationship with us. It's easier and, from our perspective, lower risk.

There are further advantages to having employees when it comes to raising investment. Investors prefer key members of your team to be employed, because they see employees as being more reliable and committed than contractors. Also, if you want to issue equity to people who contribute to your business, there are tax advantaged schemes for which only employees are eligible.

Incentivising your people

However much your employees may love working for your business, they do like to be paid. The question is, how? The three main ways of incentivising people are through money, benefits (such as generous holiday entitlements, training opportunities, and gym memberships), and equity. In a start-up you probably have limited funds available, so will potentially be considering giving away equity in exchange for salary. This has the benefits of freeing up your cash flow and of giving your people another reason to feel committed to you. Your business' success becomes their success, which gives them an added incentive to work hard and bring their best energies to their jobs.

How much equity should you give away?

Paying someone through equity means creating extra shares in your company and issuing them to a contractor, adviser, or employee. This can be in lieu of, or in addition to, a salary.

However, you need to be aware that the recipient will have to pay income tax on their value up front, just as if you'd paid them in cash. Given that the shares might be worth many thousands of pounds, this can be a disincentive, as the recipient may not have enough cash to pay the tax. And if the shares end up going down in value, the tax they paid at the beginning isn't refundable.

There are ways of getting around the tax problem which I'll go into in a moment, but one of them is to give away shares when your business is starting up and you've yet to gain any outside investment. At this stage your company has no value for tax purposes, so its shares aren't worth anything. That's not to say they won't be worth a lot in the future, but right now they're at zero and so the recipient doesn't have to pay tax until they eventually sell them.

Many founders get a bit 'equity happy' in the early stages and, in a desperate attempt to attract skills and talent into their businesses, give away huge amounts of value that they later regret. I recently discovered that one of my clients was all set to give their office manager ten percent of their business. After we'd tracked the value of the equity through various future company valuations, we worked out that those shares could end up being worth £50 million. That's a heck of a lot compared to that person's market value, and would leave a massive dent in the potential amount the founders would receive on exit. You need to think carefully about how much you give away.

None of this answers the question of *how much* equity you should part with. It's up to you, but I suggest this process as a way of calculating it. Work out what your company will probably be worth at its first investment round, then look at the value you want to give to your employee. For instance, you're onboarding Jo, a sales person. Her market rate is £50,000 a year and you're paying her £40,000, so there's a shortfall of £10,000 a year which you're making up in equity. You expect your business to be worth £1 million at its first-round valuation, so £10,000 is one percent of that. This offers you a starting point from which to move up or down. Given that you expect her to work for you for at least three years, and to make up for the inherent risk in accepting equity rather than cash, you could decide to grant her four percent.

You may be wondering what Jo's reaction would be if she's told she's receiving four percent of the business. It doesn't sound much, does it? What's more, every time new shares are issued it will dilute the percentage holding of each of the existing shareholders – including Jo's. Here's how it works:

Your business has 100 shares, held by you and your co-founder Mike, as follows:

Mike: 50 shares (50 percent)
You: 50 shares (50 percent)
TOTAL: 100 shares (100 percent)

The company takes on investment and issues ten new shares to the investor. Why new shares? Because you always issue new shares to an investor, rather than transfer existing shares. Otherwise the shares would be purchased from the existing shareholders and they, not the company, would receive the investment. Here's how it looks now:

Mike: 50 shares (45.45 percent)
You: 50 shares (45.45 percent)

Investor: 10 shares (9.01 percent)
TOTAL: 110 shares (100 percent)

You and Mike still have 50 shares each, but your percentage of the company has reduced. On the upside, the investor has ploughed money into the business so it's worth a lot more than it was before. You and Mike now own a smaller percentage of a more valuable business. If you repeat this calculation every time an employee or investor is issued shares, such as when Jo joins, you can see how the percentages would reduce in time. Each person owns a smaller percentage, but the logic is that as more investments and skills are brought into the business it should increase in value, with each shareholding also becoming more valuable.

That's why I suggest talking with employees, contractors, and co-founders about equity not in terms of percentages, but in terms of future value. Let's say, when hiring Jo, you calculate that you'll sell the company in five years' time for £50 million. You could estimate that her four percent shareholding will by then have been diluted to one percent, because of shares issued to investors and other people. However, Jo's shares would then be worth £500,000, which sounds a lot better. Of course you can't predict the future and your business may not perform as well as you imagined, but there are risks on both sides. If it does better, Jo will have a fantastic payday for a job well done.

As a side note, whenever you issue shares to your employees you need to sign a S431 election on a standard HMRC form. This locks in the tax liability between the company and the shareholder, and protects you if HMRC queries the valuation at a later date.

Two things to consider when you issue equity

We've talked about how much equity you should issue to people, but there are two other considerations as well. They are:

- ensuring that you can get the shares back if you want to; and
- further ways of delaying or reducing the tax burden on the recipient.

What this means for you and your business is what makes up the rest of this chapter.

What about getting your shares back?

When you issue shares to people who are contributing to your business' success, you're probably not thinking about wanting them back. Why would you? Your co-founder or employee is brilliantly talented and deserves to be rewarded accordingly. It will all go fantastically well.

But imagine an alternative scenario. Your co-founder and CTO, Bob, is going to develop your company's app and will be compensated with ten percent of the company's shares for his efforts. The company has only just been created, which means that the shares have no value, so you issue them to him up front. However, Bob then does nothing so you decide to take the shares back off him. Except that you can't without Bob's agreement, because they're his now. Off he swans into the sunset with potentially millions of pounds of equity in his pocket, while you're left with ten percent less of your business.

This is clearly not a good position to be in, especially if you have co-founders each with equal shares to you. Imagine if one of them was to leave the business, taking a third with them. That's why, if you're going to issue shares up front to a co-founder, employee, or anyone else, you need to have what's called a 'reverse vesting agreement'. With this in place, you issue Bob with all his shares just as before but he's deemed to earn them over time or in line with performance milestones. If he leaves the business before he's earned his shares, or doesn't perform, he keeps the ones he 'deserves' and loses the rest.

In the UK, standard vesting terms (in other words, the period over which the shares are earned) are three years, sometimes with a one-year 'cliff'. A cliff means that no shares are earned during the first year, but on the first anniversary one third of them vest in one go, with the remaining two thirds spread out over the following two years.

So how do you actually take the shares back from Bob? You can do it in one of three ways, each of which has different tax implications depending on when the shares are returned to the business:

- A share transfer from Bob to one or more other people (such as his replacement). However, this may have tax implications for the recipient.
- The company buys back the shares, perhaps at their nominal value, and either allocates them to an option pool or cancels them. However, this may have implications for future investor tax reliefs.
- The company converts the shares into a new class of 'deferred share' that has no rights (for instance,

dividend rights or the right to share in the proceeds of sale) and so has no value. Similarly to the previous option, this can cause complications for future investor tax reliefs.

As you can see, decisions about reverse vesting are not simple to make as they can have far-reaching consequences for various areas of your business – including voiding important tax reliefs for future investors. That's why, if you're putting in place a reverse vesting structure, it must be properly designed and documented. Your company may also have to pass shareholders' resolutions to make sure that it's enforceable.

Tax-friendly ways of issuing equity

I already mentioned that, when you issue shares to someone, they have to pay income tax on their value at that time. When your company is first set up the value is zero, but what about when you've been through an investment round and started trading, maybe even turning a profit? What if you were to issue shares to an employee or contractor then? At that stage the market value of the shares is calculated by reference to some complex HMRC and accounting rules, which are based on the asset value of your company, a multiple of its revenue or profit, or its latest investment round valuation.

So if, for example, your start-up has just raised investment at a £1 million valuation, it's likely that HMRC would consider the market value of the company to be £1 million. If you were to issue shares at less than their market value, the recipient would end up with a huge tax bill and would – to put it mildly – see them as a liability rather than a benefit. One solution is to grant what's known as an 'option' instead.

Options

An option is a contractual right to acquire shares at some point in the future at a pre-agreed price (which could be zero). It doesn't have to be exercised, hence why it's called an 'option'. The reason options are preferable to shares is that income tax is only payable on the market value of the shares at the point at which they're exercised (in other words, when the shares are issued). How is that better? Because in most circumstances people don't exercise their options until the company is sold. They pay a lot of tax then, but they can afford it as they're selling their shares at the same time. The only potential downside is that they'll probably pay more tax than if they'd been given the shares outright, because those shares will almost certainly have a greater market value when the business is sold than at any other point in its life cycle.

Suppose your company is valued at £1 million and you bring in a technical expert called Sam, to whom you're giving options. Here's how the tax works out:

- You give Sam five percent equity as options (valued at £50,000), which she's allowed to exercise at any time up to when the business is sold.
- You sell the company for £100 million three years later.
- At that point Sam exercises her options, and because the business has grown in value she receives shares worth £5 million. She now has to pay income tax on that.

- She therefore pays thousands of pounds in tax, but can use the proceeds of the sale of the shares to fund it.
- Sam is pretty happy.

The Enterprise Management Incentive scheme

Options are one way of granting equity in a tax-friendly way, but your team member still has to pay income tax on the value when they exercise the options and sell the shares, just like Sam did. There's another kind of option which is only applicable to employees, and which has a bigger tax advantage built in, called EMI (standing for Enterprise Management Incentive scheme). The reason it's more advantageous is that it works on a lower company valuation than normal, and may offer a lower rate of tax when the shares are sold.

EMI is quite complex and not relevant to new start-ups, so I won't go into detail here. However, it's worth looking into after you've completed an investment round or two, as it's a tax efficient way to grant options to employees.

In the next chapter we'll go through the most important legal document you'll ever draw up for your business: your customer contract.

The wrap-up

- You can't do everything yourself, but nor can you abdicate responsibility for any part of your business – try to achieve a sensible balance.
- Employees are usually more loyal, useful, and less risky to hire than contractors or advisors,

although the latter are more valuable in certain circumstances.

- When you give away equity, talk about it in terms of future value rather than percentages.
- When you issue shares, think of the tax implications for the recipients, set milestones for performance, and ensure that you can reclaim the shares if the recipient doesn't meet their obligations.

How's Lucio doing?

Earlier we learned that Lucio has recruited two co-founders: Peter his CTO and Sofia his CMO. He didn't issue shares to them at first, and still plans to remain the primary shareholder. However, now's the time for him to think about giving them some equity – it's partly why they joined his business, after all.

First he considers Peter, who he predicts will deliver consistent value over the first three years. His market rate is £75,000 a year but he's only being paid £25,000, which leaves a gap of £50,000 to be filled by equity – a total of £150,000 over three years. Lucio predicts that Pre-Train will raise its first investment round at a valuation of £1 million, which means that Peter should receive 15 percent of the business in equity.

As the company currently has no value, Lucio issues the full 15 percent up front and makes it subject to reverse vesting over three years. He also wants to make sure that Peter is as good as he says he is, so he puts in a one-year cliff, which means that Peter will receive nothing if he leaves in the first year. As soon as he reaches his first anniversary he'll get a third of the shares (five percent of the company), then the remaining ten percent in monthly instalments over the following two years.

Lucio sees the situation with Sofia a little differently. Although she's also integral to the business, she won't really be needed until the company is about to start trading. Also, her skill set is more replaceable than Peter's. Looking to the future, Lucio decides that he'll bring her in as an employee when the company closes its first investment round. Her market rate is £50,000 a year and she wants to be paid £40,000 in salary, which leaves £10,000 as an annual gap to be filled by equity. She'll probably deliver most value during the first two years rather than three, but Lucio wants to be seen to be treating her in the same way as Peter so grants her three percent vesting over three years with a one-year cliff. How has he come up with the figure of three percent? The company should be worth £1 million and there's a £30,000 gap to be filled for Sofia (her 'missing' salary for three years), so that comes to three percent of the business.

Lucio also decides that he's going to set up an identical reverse vesting schedule for himself, so that there's equal treatment for all the co-founders. As he currently owns 100 percent of the company, by the time he's given shares to Peter and Sofia he'll own 87 percent. That means he still has majority control of the business.

Chapter 5

Looking after your liabilities

Your customer contract

A couple of years ago, I received a panicked phone call from the owner of an online platform that matched personal trainers with clients – let's call it ABCTrain.com. He'd just received a VAT bill from HMRC that amounted to millions of pounds, and needless to say he had no way of paying it. What could he do?

Here was the source of his problem. People wanting a personal trainer would book and pay the trainer's fees online to ABCTrain.com (not including VAT, as none of the trainers were personally VAT registered), and ABCTrain.com would then pay the trainer after deducting ten percent commission plus VAT. This carried on for several years until HMRC started a VAT investigation into the company, originally because it spotted a couple of clerical errors in its returns. To the owner's horror, HMRC decided that ABCTrain.com should have been charging VAT not only on its commission but on the trainer's fees as well. To back up its argument, HMRC pointed out that the language in the company's business terms was unclear about who was invoicing the client for the trainers' fees, and so came to the conclusion that the business was undercharging and underpaying its VAT.

How had this lack of clarity come about? When the founder had originally set up ABCTrain.com, he'd looked around for similar platforms and found one in the US. Its website had some professional-looking terms and conditions, so he copied them and put them on his own site. However, VAT is a UK and European tax, so of course the terms were unclear about how VAT would be handled. Although on the face of it his business was identical to that of his US competitor, there were crucial technical differences in the legal provisions that were required for each. The unfortunate outcome was that, even though ABCTrain.com had been successful for many years, a few missing sentences in its terms and conditions caused it to go bust.

In ABCTrain.com's situation it was tax compliance that represented the risk to the business, but more often than not it's a company's customers. As an entrepreneur, as soon as you start selling your products or services to customers, you enter into a contract – you're committed. And while customers provide all of your revenue, they're also the area that can cause you most problems. They can sue you, trap you in an endless cycle of work that you don't want to do, and even destroy your business. Your risk is potentially unlimited.

That's unless you have a watertight customer contract in place. This is what enables you to control your risks and set the right expectations for your customers. Once your customers have agreed to a well drafted contract, not only does it protect you, it frees you up to focus on the important tasks of building your customer base, honing your products and services, and raising investment.

There are many ways of describing a customer contract – the main ones are 'customer agreement', 'terms and conditions', and 'terms of service'. But whatever name you use, it's substantially the same thing: it protects your revenue, reduces your exposure when something goes wrong, and helps your customers to understand what you will and won't do for them. And, because any relationship is a two-way street, it also lays out their obligations, such as how much (and when) they have to pay you. Of all the documents you'll create for your start-up, it's the one that's most important because it means that this crucial relationship is built on rock.

As consumers, we've become sceptical about terms and conditions (when was the last time you read those endless pages of small type when you downloaded an app or updated some software?). But terms and conditions create a legally binding contract that sets the framework for your entire business. Now you're a business owner, you need to understand what goes into this contract if you're to make sure that you're protected. What's more, the principles you'll learn apply equally to contracts with your suppliers, albeit from the opposite perspective. When you know what to look out for, you're empowered to do business with them on terms that suit you, as well as them.

In this chapter I'll explain the key elements of a customer contract. However, to protect yourself from various liabilities, you have to know what your specific risks are ahead of time, and these aren't always easy to understand. You might not predict that a certain scenario will arise, or may not know what the law says about every aspect of your business. That's why, if you decide only to use a solicitor for one thing, I strongly suggest that it's the drawing up of your customer contract. An experienced solicitor will have the knowledge to identify the risks that are specific to your business, so that you can avoid the potential nightmare of a legal action which could – in the worst cases – kill it off. It's the most important document you'll ever put in place, so it's worth doing properly.

Customer contracts – what they look like

The type of customer contract you need depends on what kind of business you run, what sort of customers you serve, and how you interact with them.

One-to-one service businesses

If you provide services to individual clients your contract will be relatively straightforward. There's only one relationship to deal with: that between you and your customer. It will most likely be a long-form contract or engagement letter that each party signs on paper or electronically.

E-commerce businesses and app providers

Here your customers are your online purchasers or users, and you'll probably call your customer contract 'terms and conditions' or 'terms of sale'. When your customers sign up to your app or go through your checkout process, they'll need to click on a link or tick a box to agree to your terms.

Software as a Service (SaaS) businesses

Customer contracts for these are more complex. Your customer is most likely a business which will use your software, and then provide its own staff or customers with access to it. You need to ask the business to sign up to your terms, but you should also consider your contractual relationship with the end users (its staff or customers). You could either make them agree to an End User Licence Agreement (EULA), or you could pass the liability for your users' activity onto your customer.

In some cases your customer might insist on the latter, especially if your software is highly tailored to their company and will only be used by their employees – they may prefer to retain control of the whole user experience themselves. However, most of the time your customers won't want to take this responsibility, and nor would you want them to. That's because you wouldn't have a contractual relationship with the end user. Suppose a user were to steal some of your IP by copying your content, and set themselves up in direct competition with you. You'd want to be able to sue them but you have no contract with them, which makes it tricky. You'd have to take action against the company (your client), and they would have to pass on their liability to the user. That isn't a great way of protecting yourself, or of maintaining good client relationships. To avoid this, it's generally best to have two contracts in place: one with your customer and one with your end users.

Platforms

Examples of these are social media sites and websites that match users with service providers. Suppose you run a platform that matches gardeners with people who want their gardens tended. Perhaps you don't charge the garden owner, but you do charge the gardener a percentage of what they earn through the site. You therefore need separate terms of service for the garden owners and the gardeners, each protecting your interests in different ways.

How your customers agree to your contract

For your customer contract to be enforceable in law you must be able to show that your customer has read it, agreed to it, and intends to be bound by it. Ideally you should do this by asking them to sign a document or tick a box online when they sign up to use your product or service, but technically any indication that they agree to the terms and intend to be bound by them is sufficient. When you can't show acceptance of a contract, you end up relying on the legal concept of 'substantial performance'. With this, if your customer receives your contract and acts as if they intend to be bound by it, they're deemed bound after a reasonable period of time.

Substantial performance is what stops someone receiving a contract, not signing it (while still allowing you to provide your products or services), and then claiming that they don't have to pay. However, if you're to persuade a judge that your customer should be bound to a contract that they haven't signed, you have to show that it was provided to them. You must also show that you flagged you'd sent it, that they understood the implications of receiving it and continuing to trade with you, and that they didn't reject or ask to amend it.

This can be difficult to demonstrate, and so it's obviously better if the contract is explicitly agreed to. There's no difference in terms of enforceability between a paper contract that's signed in pen, a virtual contract signed electronically, or terms and conditions that are agreed to online by ticking a box. Here are the main ways of securing agreement.

Online businesses: active agreement

The most legally watertight method for your online business to get agreement to your terms of service is to have them open as a pop-up. The user has to scroll all the way through before clicking an 'accept' button at the end. If there are any clauses which are particularly onerous for your user, you may want them to click to agree to them separately as well.

Your website must record:

- the version of the terms your user agreed to;
- the date and time of the agreement;
- the IP address of the user; and
- the user's username or some other way of identifying them.

An alternative is to ask the user to agree to a clear statement at the point of sign-up stating that, 'I have read and agree to the terms of service without amendment.' The terms should be linked to a web page containing them. You need to make sure that your users aren't able to complete their purchase or registration until they've ticked the box agreeing to the terms, otherwise they could argue that they didn't know the content of them.

Online businesses: passive agreement

Some online platforms have a statement at sign-up stage that says, 'By clicking "submit" I agree to be bound by the terms of service.' This is risky as the user can claim that they didn't read the terms, especially if they're not hyperlinked or easily available. Even more problematic is to put a link to your terms at the bottom of your website, with no reference to them at all during the checkout process. In almost all circumstances, this won't be an adequate way of binding your customers to your terms.

Link in an email

In certain industries such as recruitment, it's common to reference terms by way of a link in an email. This only works if your email draws the reader's attention to it, and if your terms aren't particularly onerous for the recipient. Most recruitment terms contain potentially onerous provisions, such as that if a candidate introduced by the recruiter is hired, a fee is payable. If the reader of the email can show they weren't aware of, and didn't agree to, the recruiter's fee, they can argue that the terms aren't binding.

Signed document

These are most common with one-to-one services businesses such as solicitors, architects, or financial advisers. Lots of things can go wrong, particularly when you're giving advice. You want people to have a detailed understanding of what they're signing up to, so a written contract which can be signed on paper or electronically works best.

Order form

If your business uses physical order forms, you can put your terms on the back or attach them to the form. Just make sure that you have a clear statement on the front that's signed by your customer, stating that they've read and agreed the terms.

How to decide?

You can see that there's a balance to strike between how interruptive the method of getting agreement to your customer contract is to your sign-up process, and how much risk you bear if it's not legally binding. This is especially the case if you're an online business. You'll probably have to balance the desires of your user experience (UX) developers (who'd rather have no formal agreement to your terms) and your solicitor (who wants the agreement to be as explicit as possible). My view is that for most moderate value online purchases you just want your customers to click and buy, but for a one-to-one customer buying something expensive or highly tailored you want them to understand the contract and have the opportunity to discuss it.

It comes down to your attitude to risk. How likely is it that your customers will be put off from buying if they have to read and agree to your terms first? On the other hand, what are the potentially negative consequences if they sign up to something that they don't understand? If your terms are pretty standard and the risk of a judge deciding that your customer isn't bound by them are low, you can perhaps use less robust methods in your sign-up process. But if some of your terms are complex or onerous, for instance if your customers have to pay high cancellation fees, you need to make sure that they've read them properly.

A final point on agreeing to contracts: all of the above also applies when you *change* them. As a general rule, merely updating the link to your terms of service on your website without telling anyone isn't sufficient for your customers to be bound by them. You also need to draw their attention to the changes, and maybe even gain an acceptance from them as well.

What you promise to deliver

Part of the purpose of your customer contract is to set out your obligations to your customers. This is as much for your benefit as theirs, because it allows you to clarify what you are and aren't agreeing to do. Customers will almost always push the envelope when it comes to the scope of your work, and this is much easier for them to get away with if you haven't drawn the boundaries up front.

You know your business and the way you work, but your client doesn't. I take the view that it's your job to lay out what you will and won't do, so that your clients are clear from the outset. You'll also be doing yourself a lot of favours in the process.

Suppose you're a graphic designer and agree to design a company's logo for a fixed fee of £500. You come up with three designs, but your client doesn't like any of them and suggests something different. You design three further options, from which they choose one but ask for numerous revisions. Twenty versions later they agree to the design, and a project you anticipated would take five hours has taken twenty-five. You could have pre-empted this by specifying in your agreement a set number of proposals and revisions – you'd have been setting expectations early so that everyone understood what was included.

What your customers promise to deliver

Although you're the provider of your goods or services, your customer may have to help in some way so that you can deliver them. You need to be clear about what you expect for them, and what happens if they don't play their part. Let's say you're the graphic designer again. When you start working with a new client to design their logo, you need a full brief from them and feedback on your work. If they don't give you that information in a timely manner, you'll be hard pressed to create the logo they want.

Sound customer contracts should therefore contain your client's obligations, and clauses defining what happens if they don't meet them. If they don't give you what you need by the time that's agreed, you can charge for any additional hours you take working on the project as a result.

Using your customer contract to get paid

One of the main reasons for having a customer contract is to make sure that you're paid for your work, so it's important that you make your charges clear. You don't want to end up in a situation in which your customer is able to argue that they thought they were paying one fee, whereas you thought they were paying another.

Unfortunately, at some point you might have to deal with a customer who refuses to pay for what you've delivered, and you end up taking them to the small claims court (which, by the way, is pretty easy). For your claim to succeed you'll have to show the judge two things: that you sent a formal demand for payment (an invoice) and that the date you set for payment has passed and the payment hasn't been made. What's more, the payment deadline should be specified both in your customer contract and on the invoice. If you don't have these pieces of evidence the judge won't rule in your favour, even if it's obvious that you're in the right.

By the way, the law says you can charge interest on overdue commercial debts at a rate of eight percent above the base rate of the Bank of England. I always advise including a clause to that effect into your customer contract, because it's far more effective to point to the clause than to a piece of legislation (the name of which you can never remember when the time comes).

Refunds

Your customer contract should be clear about your refund policy. However, if you sell goods this isn't entirely up to you, as UK law sets out the following rules:

- If an item is faulty, not as described, or doesn't do what it's supposed to, you must offer a full refund.
- You don't have to offer a refund if the customer:
  - knew the item was faulty when they bought it;
  - damaged it by trying to repair it themselves (though they may still have a right to a partial refund);
  - asked for it to be personalised (unless it's faulty); or
  - no longer wants it, unless they bought it without seeing it (see below).

When a customer buys something online, by mail order, or by telephone, this is known as 'distance selling'. In this case, subject to certain exceptions, they have the right to return their order for a refund for a limited time, even if the goods aren't faulty.

Term and termination

The word 'term' describes the lifespan of your customer contract, and 'termination' is the moment when you (or your customer) ends it. When you set up a new customer contract you might not be thinking about how long you want it to carry on for – in fact, you may be assuming that it goes on forever. That isn't how it works, because contracts always need a term if they're to be legally enforceable. It's possible to have a 'rolling contract' which automatically renews each year, such as you'd create if you were an app or software developer, but in that case you'd need a clause that says it will renew unless one of the parties gives notice to terminate.

The other point to be aware of is that you mustn't have unfair provisions in your term and termination clauses. Suppose you run a subscription service which costs your customers £100 a month. You put in place a one-year minimum contract term, which renews automatically for another year unless your customer gives a month's notice. Naturally many of your customers forget to terminate, and find they're stuck with another year's service which they don't want but still have to pay for. In this situation you run the risk of your terms being considered unfair, which could invalidate your entire contract.

If your customer wants to terminate the contract

Your contract has to be clear about how people can cancel it. If yours is a service business, you'll usually state that if your client changes their mind about working with you they can only terminate by giving a certain period of notice. They then have to pay for all the services they've received to date, or a pre-agreed portion. It's important to think about this, because if a customer cancels your service part way through you've lost the future income from it. You can't impose a penalty for termination because that's not legally enforceable, but what you can do is to pre-agree something called 'liquidated damages'. With this, you state that if the customer terminates early it's understood that your loss will be a certain amount (which has to be a genuine estimate). Although this might be the same figure as a penalty, and therefore amounts to the same thing to you, to the law it's more enforceable.

Some service businesses run into problems when their customers reject their work on the basis that it's not up to standard. If this happens to you it's important that you have the chance to correct the errors, and only if what you've delivered hasn't been altered by anyone else (this is key for software and app developers). So you build an acceptance mechanism into your contract, in which your customer has a set time period to accept or reject your deliverable. This should include the process for acceptance, the criteria for it, and how long it will take. If they don't reject the work, or if they start using it, they're deemed to have accepted it. This creates an easy default to ensure that you're paid.

If you want to terminate the contract

What happens if you want to terminate a contract with a customer, rather than the other way around? As a start-up you're probably more focused on building up your customer base than reducing it, but there are times when you might want to stop working with someone. It could be that you signed up a client in the early days who isn't paying you much or is a pain to work with, and now you want to move on. For this, you need to have a provision in your contract that allows you to terminate by giving notice.

If your customer doesn't pay you

I referred earlier to what you'll need as proof in the small claims court if a customer doesn't pay you, but it's also important to understand how you can guard against this in your contract. You might assume that you can just stop providing your goods or services, but it's not as simple as that. Let's say you're a PR agency, and your client pays you a retainer of £1,000 a month in arrears. In March they fail to pay your invoice, so you down tools. The relationship ends in court, where you ask the judge to award you the overdue £1,000 plus interest, but your client counterclaims for £5,000 by arguing that you breached the contract by refusing to do any more work. In fact, they say your services are so amazing that the loss from the benefit they would have gained is £10,000, so now you owe them £9,000! This might sound outrageous and is, frankly, one of the areas in which the law can appear to be rather irrational, but a court could well find in your client's favour. Your way out of this nightmare is to include a standard termination clause in your contract. This says if you're not paid within a certain time period, you can either suspend work or terminate entirely.

A similar concept applies if you have a business customer who gets into financial trouble. If an administrator is appointed to take over the management of their company, it can pick and choose which contracts it wants to continue with. Should its beady eyes alight on yours it can force you to continue working for your client, even though (given that it's in administration) you may well not be paid. To forestall this, you should include a clause stating that in the case of your customer becoming insolvent you can immediately terminate the contract.

Protecting your intellectual property with your contract

We've already talked about how important it is that your valuable IP is owned by your company rather than by your co-founders or suppliers. However, IP protection also has a place in your customer contract because it prevents your users and customers from copying it. How you go about this depends on what kind of business you own.

One-to-one service businesses

This is straightforward. All you need is a clear statement in your customer agreement that you're the owner or licensor of the IP that you use in your service. Alternatively you might want to transfer the IP you create for your client to them, as you probably would if you were designing their advert or writing their website copy. The point is that it's your IP and you can decide what to do with it.

Web, software, or app developer businesses

In this case you may have up to five different types of IP to take into account. Your customer contract should set out the relevant categories and what's included in each.

- **Multi-use, proprietary IP** belonging to you. This is code that you've already produced and used for multiple clients so you don't have to re-create the basics from scratch. You need to grant a licence of this IP to your client, potentially with some restrictions.

- **Third party IP**, such as WordPress software or source code for widgets created by someone else. You'll probably need to ensure that your customer purchases the licence to this IP themselves.

- **IP in open-source software**. Different open-source softwares have different rules. Many require that you state in your terms of service the licence under which it's used, and give a link to the long-form licence. A small number specify that the code in any website or platform using their software becomes open source in itself. This means that the entire code of the website or app that you develop can be used by anyone else.

- **Client IP**, such as your client's logo and content, which you incorporate into the website or app that you're developing. Your agreement should state that you have a licence to use it solely for the purposes of providing your services.

- **Custom IP**, which is IP in the product or deliverables created by you – simplistically, it's everything that's not covered by the other categories of IP. You and your client need to agree who will own it. You should only agree to transfer your custom IP once your client has paid for all your services, and your terms should state that. Flipping the coin, if you're the client it's important to review this clause very carefully indeed. You should take particular note of the timing of the custom IP transfer, and think about what would happen if you have a dispute with its creator. Would none of the IP transfer to you if you refuse to pay for all of the services?

Your data privacy obligations

The next chapter explains how to ensure that you're compliant with data privacy legislation, but in the context of your customer contract it's worth flagging up some points that will help you to limit your liability should anything go wrong. This is important, because while the terms of your contract can't stop the regulator from fining you, they can still go a long way towards limiting what you have to pay out if your customer were to take legal action against you.

First, it's important to recognise that a data breach can result in your customer or client suffering a significant loss – a loss for which they might sue you. For instance, our friend Lucio plans to process personal data about prospective candidates on behalf of his corporate clients. Imagine if there were to be a data breach in which confidential information was leaked to one of his client's competitors – that could be hugely damaging for Lucio's client. This is why you need to cap your liability for data breaches.

Second, you should also try to exclude as much liability as possible. If yours is an online business it's standard to include a statement that, while you take reasonable steps to protect users' data, it's submitted at their risk. You'll also want to ensure that your users protect their login information, so that any misuse of their password is their responsibility.

Insurance

We looked at the importance of insurance before, but it's worth considering whether your customers will require you to have insurance in place. Likewise, ask yourself if you require your customers to have insurance, and whether this should go into your terms. Suppose you run a platform that connects homeowners who have spare attic space with people who have storage needs. You take the payment from the people who need the space, and send a proportion of it to the homeowners. Because you operate the platform, users could try to sue you for any problems caused by the homeowners, such as a burst pipe damaging the stored possessions. You need to make sure that the homeowners have insurance to cover a third party's belongings, and this should go into your terms of service.

Limiting your liability

Without a limitation of liability clause in your contract, you potentially have unlimited liability if something goes wrong. This clause is how you control the level of your potential losses, and while it's not the most exciting aspect of your agreement it's certainly the most important.

What you can't exclude

In English law (as in most jurisdictions) you can't exclude liability for death or personal injury caused by gross negligence or fraud by you or your business. You should always include a statement to this effect in your limitation of liability clause, because if you don't it can invalidate the entire clause. There are also, depending on your type of business, certain statutory provisions that you can't contract out of. You need to know what these are, and state that you don't seek to exclude them.

What you can exclude

The good news is that in law you can exclude liability for most other types of risk, and it's important that it's clear that you've done this in your contract because there are multiple losses that your customers can potentially claim for. There are also certain types of risk that you could exclude liability for, but might decide not to. Instead, you can cap your liability. This is what we explored in Chapter 2, when we talked about being on the hook for a certain amount of your client's losses if it helps you to win the work.

Although it might seem like a great idea to exclude liability for whatever you can, I have a word of warning about this. There's both legislation and a wealth of case law designed to protect your customers against unfair contractual terms. So ask yourself if your limitation of liability clause is objectively fair, and if you come to the conclusion that it's pretty aggressive compared to the market standard, you need to do everything you can to flag it to your client so they understand the implications. This is particularly the case when there's an inequality of bargaining power and your customer is in a weaker position than you, in which case you may want to ask them to seek independent legal advice.

If you don't take these steps, you may find that your limitation of liability clause is unenforceable. For instance, imagine if my legal firm were to exclude liability for negligence, so that if we gave people the wrong advice we wouldn't be held responsible in any way. And imagine if we had a clause to this effect in our customer contract but didn't draw it to our clients' attention. Given that our job is to advise them on legal issues, it's not unreasonable to assume that some of them may not read this clause. It's objectively unfair for us to have no liability whatsoever if we give wrong advice, and if we were to be taken to court by a client on this basis a judge would strike out the exclusion of liability and impose something more reasonable.

The importance of indemnities

This is techy legal stuff, but it's useful to understand what an indemnity is and what it does, because many people (including some solicitors) don't know. It's easiest to understand through an example.

Suppose you pay your marketing agency to run an online campaign for you, but part way through you cancel your contract without giving the required notice. This causes the agency a financial loss, but for it to sue you it has to show a judge three things: that it's suffered a loss and can quantify it; that the loss resulted directly from your breach of contract; and that it's taken reasonable steps to minimise it (for instance by seeking work elsewhere). That might be difficult to do. The loss may not have fully materialised yet, it might only have been partly caused by your breach of contract, or the agency may not want to spend time and money on finding other work.

However, if the agency had insisted on an indemnity clause its life would be much easier, because an indemnity gets around many of these issues. With an indemnity claim there's no need for the agency to prove fault or negligence on your part, only to show that the 'trigger' for the indemnity has happened – in this case, your breach of contract. It also doesn't have to mitigate its loss.

That's why large companies may ask you to indemnify them against any loss they suffer that's caused by you, as part of your customer contract with them. As you can see, an indemnity makes it more likely that you'll end up paying your customer, and paying them a greater sum, if something goes wrong. You should therefore be very careful about agreeing to one.

Boilerplate clauses

We solicitors always add in a number of standard clauses at the end of contracts. Although we enjoy a good clause, we don't do this for the fun of it, but because they're important. The key ones that you almost always need to include are:

- **Governing law:** the laws of the country that will apply in the event of a dispute. This is particularly important if your customers may not be based in England and Wales.

- **Jurisdiction:** the location of the courts in which any litigation would be heard. Would you rather be sued in the UK, or Kenya?
- **Notices:** how either party can send legal notices. This is important in the event of termination or litigation.
- **Third party rights:** did you know that, by default, your customer's spouse, civil partner, child, parent, or legal representative could bring a claim against you? Let's imagine that you sell your customer Julia a door for her mum Linda's house, and someone breaks down the door and steals her handbag. Linda could try to sue you. To avoid this, you can put a clause in your contract saying that only the parties to the contract can sue – in other words, Julia. In this case, Julia may have suffered no loss that you're responsible for, and so can't claim.

In the next chapter we'll go through the fundamentals of GDPR and data protection law, so you can create a positive relationship with your customers and avoid being sued.

The wrap-up

- Without a well-worded (and agreed to) customer contract in place, your liability to your customers is potentially unlimited.
- Your customer contract sets the framework for your whole business, so if you're only going to pay a solicitor to draw up one document, make it this one.

- Customer contracts set out (amongst other things) both parties' obligations to each other, how the contract can be terminated, the IP that's protected, and how your liability can be limited.
- They can take various forms and be agreed to in different ways, depending on what kind of business you have.

How's Lucio doing?

Lucio can see that his SaaS business, Pre-Train, has a potentially complex legal relationship with its customers and users, so he's keen to make sure that this is well handled in his customer contract. He doesn't feel confident that he can do it himself, so he goes to his solicitor to make sure that all eventualities are catered for.

His solicitor tells him that, as far as his corporate clients are concerned, Lucio needs a 'software as a service' agreement drawn up specifically for them. Lucio has struck lucky more quickly than he'd expected, and is currently in negotiation with his first major customer, an investment bank. The bank wants to make sure that if Lucio's software fails for any reason, he's liable for the losses. It rejects Lucio's draft limitation of liability clause in which Pre-Train seeks to avoid any liability, so Lucio's solicitor recommends a £1 million cap. He now needs to insure against this, just in case the worst happens.

Also, the bank is concerned about how the personal data of the platform's users will be protected – these are the bank's potential future employees, after all. It has said that it wants Lucio to indemnify the bank for any liability it may have as a result of Pre-Train breaching the contract's confidentiality clause. Lucio decides that as this is the only way the bank will sign the contract he'll agree, although he won't do it for most of his clients. It's important for the start-up's credibility that it has a major client on board.

As regards Pre-Train's users, Lucio wants a direct contractual relationship with them because he needs to have direct recourse if they copy his IP or upload unlawful or offensive content. So he asks his solicitor to draw up an end user licence agreement, which each user has to agree to by ticking a box before they can create an account. The key elements of it are that it explains how to use the platform, and also what happens to the content users upload. It also explains what they're not allowed to upload, that Pre-Train owns the IP in the platform, and that the recruiters' training materials belong to them, not the users. Finally, the agreement states that Lucio has the right to terminate the contract immediately if the user breaches any of the terms.

Chapter 6

Understanding data protection law

Use it to your advantage

There's nothing more likely to elicit a groan from the previously enthusiastic entrepreneur than the thought of complying with data protection law. I understand why – it sometimes feels like a tick box exercise. And who wants to be 'compliant' anyway? You didn't become an entrepreneur to follow the rules, but so you could do something different and exciting.

However, getting to grips with the principles and processes of data protection is one of those things that – once you understand it – can help you to *win* customers. Being compliant encourages you to put yourself in their shoes. You're asking yourself: 'What would I like to see in a business to which I'm giving my personal data? What would convince me that they're trustworthy?' This process can help you to build a more customer-friendly business. And it goes without saying that you don't want to be fined or sued – that could be disastrous, not only for your finances but for your reputation.

For these reasons, this chapter will focus as much on the process you need to go through if you're to be data compliant, as it will the technicalities of data protection law.

It will help you to understand your risks, decide which data to collect and the best way of processing it, and outline what documentation you need to draw up.

What is personal data?

First of all, although your focus is probably on GDPR (or the General Data Protection Regulation, to give its more catchy name), it's important to know that there are actually a lot of different laws, rules, and guidance that come into play when it comes to personal data. The GDPR is an EU regulation that was implemented into UK law in 2018 by the Data Protection Act of the same year. The UK has now left the EU but that doesn't exempt it from complying with GDPR, as I'll explain later. However, UK-GDPR is only one aspect of a far wider set of rules. There are additional rules that cater for the use of cookies, marketing activities, and a range of other data-related elements.

When we talk about data protection rules, we're thinking about the rules that apply to the use of personal data. This is any information that relates to an 'identifiable natural person', and includes (among other things) their:

- name;
- address;
- email address;
- date of birth; and
- health and medical information.

Personal data also covers information that's collected when users access your website, app, or software, and includes their geolocation data, cookie records, and user ID. There used to be a distinction between business and personal data, but that no longer exists. So a business email address is counted as personal data as long as it isn't a generic one, such as an info@address.

What if personal data is anonymised, for instance if you were to publish the total number of users of your app? It then stops being personal data, so the obligations of GDPR don't apply. However, it's important to understand what anonymisation actually means. When something is anonymised, nobody can identify any individuals from that data. But if anyone (including the person who anonymised the data) can break it down to identify the people to whom it relates, that data is what's called 'pseudonymised'.

For instance, a doctor sends a patient's blood sample to a lab for analysis. The sample is allocated a number, rather than the name of the patient. The lab can't figure out the identity of the patient, but the doctor can match the sample number with their records, so the data is pseudonymised. This kind of data is still personal data, and must be processed in accordance with GDPR.

You need to think about the legal basis for processing people's personal data. In the past, a lot of businesses relied on asking users to tick a box consenting to everything set out in the company's privacy policy. GDPR changed that approach, as consent is now only valid if the data subject gives a positive affirmation of consent, such as signing an agreement, ticking an unchecked tick box, or clicking an 'I agree' button. In addition, you need to ask for separate consent for each and every use of their personal data, making it clear what they're agreeing to. For instance, if you want your users to consent to receiving marketing communications, to the transfer of their data to your sister company based in the US, and to the sale of their data, you potentially need three separate consents. This is a great way to cause a huge drop-off in your sign-up pathway and to give your user experience designers a nervous breakdown.

Because of this, most businesses explore other legal ways of processing personal data. Here are the most common ones:

- **Contractual performance:** you need to process the data in order to provide your goods and services. For instance, if you have an e-commerce store you need your customers' addresses to send them what they've bought.
- **Legal obligation:** for example, if you run a bank you have to verify the identity of new account applicants.
- **Legitimate interest:** you have what's called a 'legitimate interest' in processing the personal data. This seems like a catch-all, but it's only valid if the processing doesn't interfere with the 'fundamental rights and freedoms' of the individual. For instance, you provide tailored training to restaurants on complying with food safety standards. A restaurant owner downloads an information sheet from your website by entering their email address. You have a legitimate interest in sending them an email asking if they'd like further information about your services – in other words, you're entitled to assume that they're interested in them. However, if you were to add them to your email marketing database without their permission and send them a daily

marketing email, you don't meet the requirement of legitimate interests because your spam interferes with their fundamental rights and freedoms.

'Data subjects', as they're called, have many rights under GDPR. These include the right to ask for a copy of all personal data held about them (a 'subject access request'), the right to object to direct marketing, the right to have their personal data erased, and the right to object to being made subject to automated decision making. It's important to think through how you'll allow for the exercise of these rights, and to what extent they apply to your business.

The key principles of GDPR

When it comes to data protection, you don't need to understand all the ins and outs of the regulations (and if you want to, there are whole books written on the topic). What's most helpful is to know about the basic principles, because then you can work out how they apply to your start-up.

GDPR sets out six principles that you must comply with.

1. Lawfulness, fairness, and transparency

When you process people's personal data, ask yourself if you're operating under this principle. Could any of your customers or users claim that they're not aware of how you're using their data, that they feel exploited in any way, or that you're not complying with the law? If you're fulfilling this first principle you're a long way towards ensuring that your customers are happy.

2. Purpose

You must only collect and process data for specified, explicit, and legitimate purposes. That means you must be able to explain to people why you're collecting their data, and what you intend to do with it (and then not do completely different things with it).

3. Minimisation

You must only collect data that's adequate, relevant, and limited to what's necessary in relation to its purposes. In other words, you should only ask for the data that you need and retain it for as long as you need it and no longer.

I find that many entrepreneurs, in their eagerness to maximise their marketing opportunities, collect all the data they think they may ever want. Suppose you sell party products online, what data do you strictly need? It would only be your customers' names, addresses, delivery addresses, and probably their email addresses. But suppose you have plans to send marketing emails to specific types of customers, such as those who identify as gay – maybe you have a plan to promote your Pride weekend decorations. So you have the bright idea of asking for their sexuality in your checkout or registration process. This causes you three problems. First, sexuality is 'special category data', and imposes a much higher obligation on you in terms of data security. This gives you a technical headache. Second, given the sensitive nature of the data you may need explicit consent (which is separate from any other consent) to use it . This interrupts your checkout process. And third, few people want to volunteer private information like this to a party products site and may go elsewhere instead. This causes you to lose customers. A better option would be to set up a Pride weekend marketing campaign, in which you ask people to sign up to a special list, then market the party goods to them that way.

4. Accuracy

The data must be accurate and up to date, and if it's not, you need to correct or delete it. That means that you should have a process in place to periodically update the data you hold.

5. Storage

You shouldn't keep or process personal data for longer than is necessary for the purposes for which you collected it. This is an area which business owners often don't think through. The longer you store data, the more risk you have of it ending up in the wrong hands. If there's no real benefit in hanging onto it, why take the chance?

I recently reviewed a client's privacy policy. They have an app that helps people who've been injured, and had drawn up a privacy policy (worryingly, with the help of a legal privacy expert) that said they'd retain all medical data for 50 years! Health data is special category data and has a whole bunch of extra rules associated with it, so I suggested that they keep it for one year after the user has stopped interacting with the app, then email to say they'll delete it unless there's an objection.

6. Integrity and confidentiality

You must keep people's data secure. Goes without saying, I guess.

In summary, when you're planning your business, think about what personal data you need and why. It isn't permissible to collect all the data you might possibly want in the future and keep it forever.

What to do

Data protection compliance is a process – it's something you do in stages. It can feel overwhelming when you think about all the things you could tackle, but in most cases you don't have to do it all, and certainly not at the beginning. You can summarise your actions into two key steps:

1. Decide what risk profile you fall into and take the steps appropriate to that.
2. Draw up your documentation.

I'll cover the risk analysis here and in the next section I'll walk you through the documentation side of things.

Assessing the risk

The main idea behind GDPR is that it reduces the risk of people's personal data being misused in any way. Your job as a founder is therefore to understand the risks that holding the data may give rise to, and to take the right steps to minimise them. Your risk profile depends on what sector you're in, what kind of data you need to collect, and how you plan to use it. If you run a low-risk business it wouldn't make sense for you to spend the same amount of time and money on GDPR compliance as a high-risk business.

As a starting point to work out your risk level, imagine a nightmare scenario: a hacker gains access to your secure servers and therefore to your customers' personal data. What would be the impact of the data breach?

Suppose you're a cake shop on the high street. If the hackers manage to harvest your customers' email addresses, they might send them phishing emails trying to con them out of money in some way. You'd have to notify your customers (and potentially the regulator), who might not be happy with you, but the risk of harm is relatively low. For you as a business, therefore, you can take a standard approach to GDPR compliance planning. All you need at first is a well-thought-through privacy policy that explains to your customers why you're collecting their data and what you'll do with it. Then, as the business grows, you might want to ask a solicitor to revise it and make sure it's watertight.

On the other hand, suppose you're a cancer clinic giving diagnostic and treatment services to sick people. As well as names and contact details, you have all sorts of sensitive and personal data on your servers to do with your clients' health, the drugs they're on, and maybe their race, sexuality, and personal circumstances. You may also hold data on their families, and the insurance companies they're with. The harm that a hacker could inflict with that collection of data in their hands is extreme, to say nothing of the fact that they'd potentially be attacking vulnerable people who are going through a difficult time in their lives.

For you as a business, therefore, you'd need to prioritise your security measures and have robust procedures to detect and prevent hacking attempts. Unlike the cake shop, you wouldn't just create your own privacy policy and hope for the best, you'd consult a solicitor from day one to make sure it's done properly. You'd also ask IT experts to advise you on your data security and map out the journey your customers' data will go on once it's collected. Then, as your company grows, you'd build on that.

Unless you own a high-risk business you don't have to be 100 percent compliant from day one, with every box ticked. It's far more important to understand your risk profile and have the documentation in place that shows you're compliant, so your customers feel confident in buying from you. You can worry about the more difficult stuff, such as putting in place background documentation, as you go along.

The documents you need to draw up

Many founders think that GDPR compliance is only about having the right documentation, but it's not. It's about the process – the analysis, the thinking, and the setting up of procedures and rules that ensure your business is compliant all the time. The documents are there to reflect what you actually do, otherwise they're not worth anything.

So what documentation do you need? For most businesses, there are four items:

- **Data protection impact assessment.** This records your 'thinking' – it's like a risk assessment. Many start-ups skip this but it's the most important stage of your data protection compliance. It records what data you process, what you do with it, and on what basis. Not only does it help you to focus on this area, but you'll also need it if you have to prove that you've given proper thought to it.

- **Privacy policy.** This is the public-facing document that tells your customers and users what you'll do with their data. I've given this its own section next.
- **Data processing agreement.** When you hand personal data to a third party to be processed on your customers' behalf, this document sets out how you'll do it and what both parties' obligations are.
- **Background documentation.** This details your internal processes, such as policies, risk assessments, and staff training materials.

Your privacy policy

Customers are increasingly wary about how companies use their personal data, so it makes sense to think through how you present your data processing activities to them. They should feel reassured when they read your privacy policy, and be able to understand why you're collecting their data and what you're going to do with it.

This is even more important for special category data. As an example, I use an online GP service which has access to my medical records and other private information about me. When I signed up to the app, I took special care to read the privacy policy and was impressed by how well written it was. It told me that the company would only disclose my data to my GP, and even then only with my explicit consent on each occasion. Also, I can delete the data they hold by clicking a button on the site. That's important to me, and I suspect I wouldn't be the only person signing up for this kind of service who wants to know this information.

It's important to realise that, depending on what kind of business you own, you may have clients who are extra vigilant about your privacy policy if you're processing data about *their* customers. I was approached for help by the owner of a company that provided SaaS products for businesses in the health care space. When he'd originally set up his platform, he'd downloaded a privacy policy template from an off-the-shelf website and used it for almost two years. This would have been risky enough, but in addition to that, he hadn't done any of the analysis that the law requires or taken advice on his GDPR compliance. As part of a routine review by his biggest client, he was asked some questions about his company's compliance with the outcome of the Schrems case. 'Schrems?' he replied. 'What do you mean by that?' Schrems is some litigation that invalidated a US-EU regime on data security equivalency between the two jurisdictions. The fact that he'd never heard of it set alarm bells ringing for his client, who proceeded to dive into the rest of the company's data protection analysis with renewed vigour. The client ended up cancelling their contract, and it took £15,000 and three months for the business owner to resolve all the issues. The cost of setting it up properly in the first place, and keeping it under review, would have been a fraction of that.

Marketing using personal data

This can be a key concern. What you can and can't do is governed by UK-GDPR, along with other UK regulations, so it's worth asking for legal advice on your plans to market your business. These are the high-level guidelines to get you started:

- You can send marketing communications to your current and recent clients, as long as the emails have an unsubscribe option and the recipients haven't already unsubscribed.
- You can usually send marketing communications to your leads, as long as they've interacted with you in some way. However, you can only send them relevant information, and any emails must have an unsubscribe option.
- Don't buy marketing lists, as the people on them may not have consented to receiving anything from you.

The key to generating effective and compliant marketing leads is to get people to interact with you. Run marketing campaigns, publish content on social media, and hold events – these will all yield valuable contact details which you're free to use appropriately.

What about Brexit?

The question on everyone's lips: do we still have to abide by GDPR now that the UK has left the EU? The answer is, 'mainly yes'.

To understand why, it's helpful to know that before Brexit the UK had its own version of GDPR which was similar to the EU version. This is the one we're following now, but it only applies to the processing of data in the UK about people based in the UK. If your company processes data about people based in the EU, if it has an EU presence such as a company office there, or if it targets people based in the EU, these processing activities become subject to EU-GDPR. Bear in mind that this applies if you sell goods or services to people in the EU, such as through your website, or if you monitor the behaviour of people in the EU, for instance through cookies on your site.

If that's the case for you, you may now need to appoint an EU representative located in the EU. This is a person, company, or organisation who can represent your business to EU regulators. However, there's a legal get-out from this if your data processing is both 'occasional' and unlikely to risk the safety of a person's data protection rights and freedoms.

That concludes this part of the book, in which we've explored the process of setting up a business and getting it ready to launch. In the next part we'll dive into raising investment, starting with a tour of the investment landscape.

The wrap-up

- Being data protection compliant can help you to win customers and avoid being fined or sued.
- If you understand and comply with the principles of GDPR, you'll have a customer-friendly and well protected business.

- Data protection compliance is a process: assess your risks, take appropriate action, and create the right documentation.
- You probably don't have to do all this in one go.

How's Lucio doing?

From the discussions he's had with his solicitor about his customer contract, Lucio knows that data protection is a relatively high-risk area for him. If his business takes off he'll have thousands of users on his database, and the risk to his reputation and financial security if his clients were to sue because of a data breach could be catastrophic. So he goes through a risk assessment process and documents everything. After that, he takes legal advice.

He focuses first on his corporate clients. His company will be processing their job applicants' data, so he needs to have a data processing agreement with them. In this, his clients commit to passing on the personal data of their potential recruits, which he'll process on their behalf. It sets out how he does that and what security measures he has in place – this is crucial for winning his clients' trust.

In creating this document, he starts thinking about the classes of data that he'll be handling. At first he reckons that it would be a good idea to collect information about the applicants' education history and qualifications, and any health problems that might affect their ability to do a job. This is in line with his aims to make the platform a socially responsible one. But not only would that give people extra fields to fill in, the inclusion of special category data (the health data) would also give him a security headache. So he decides to leave collecting that kind of information to his clients, thereby minimising what he'll hold himself. He can always run surveys with his clients and users if he wants to track how well applicants from disadvantaged backgrounds are doing.

Next he turns his attention to his users, the job applicants. His privacy policy is the relevant document here, which he asks his solicitor to draw up. He then enters a reference to it in his end user licence agreement. Data-wise, he's all set for now.

PART TWO

Raising investment

Chapter 7

Where to find funding

The investment landscape

There comes a moment in the life of most start-ups when they need to raise money. You may have been funding your venture using your own savings, or have brought in co-founders who've given their work and expertise for free. You might even have raised some early stage funding already and be thinking about the next step. This chapter lays out the different sources of funding so that you can start thinking about your options. I've broken them down into:

- early stage equity funding;
- later stage equity funding;
- crowdfunding;
- loans; and
- grants.

In the following chapter I'll show you how to value your company (the first step towards raising investment), and in the one after that I'll give you some essential advice on when to approach investors and how to do it.

Before I go any further, it's worth highlighting something that relates to the geographical spread of funding opportunities in the UK. There's a significant difference between London and the rest of the country, with a noticeable amount more money available in the capital. That's not surprising, I guess – it's the main investment hub for much of Europe now – but it does mean that raising funds in London is a more straightforward process than elsewhere. The main exception is Manchester, which seems to have attracted most of the investors in the north. There are also key investment hubs around Oxford, Cambridge, and Warwick, where you'll find early stage funds for sectors such as biotech. This means that if your business isn't based in London, you'll probably still need to network the London investment market because it's where you'll find the majority of opportunities. That's especially the case when you're looking to raise larger equity rounds.

How to find investors

This is the big question that I'm most often asked. When I set up Buckworths I was a new entrepreneur, and nervous about what potential clients would think of a guy who'd quit his job at one of the world's top law firms to work with start-up businesses. After all, my main experience had been with billion-pound mergers and acquisitions, not with fledgling companies. After burying my head in my marketing strategy and barely speaking to anyone in the first few months, I realised I had to get out there and network, so I started speaking at events for entrepreneurs. To my relief I soon found that new business owners were delighted to work with a law firm that specialised in helping them, rather than with a bigger firm that would treat them as a low priority. What's more, I discovered from those conversations that some of the things I'd assumed were important to founders actually weren't, and I adapted my business accordingly.

Now, ten years later, I have a personal network of over 20,000 start-up founders and service providers, many of whom have been generous enough to refer me to new clients and be supportive of my firm. My experience is that fellow founders are often happy to share their contacts and make introductions to investors when they can. This shows how important having a network is for raising funds. Without one you'll be relying on 'cold' outreach, which can work but is certainly more difficult and time-consuming.

From today, your job as a founder is to work on building your own network. The most successful entrepreneurs talk about their businesses all the time, building relationships with investors whom they can tap up when needed. I suggest telling anyone who'll listen about your venture, because by sharing your ideas you'll get to know more people, create connections, and one day get someone excited enough about your business to invest in it.

Networking doesn't only take place at events. Not long after I set up Buckworths, a friend introduced a potential client to me. The guy's business idea was, shall we say, unusual. It was to set up a website for people who liked dressing up as cats and attending 'purr' parties, at which (I can only assume) they'd purr at each other. It even sold cat masks and other weird-looking paraphernalia. I suppose it was 'purr-fect' if you're into that kind of thing. To my surprise he already had an investor on board – a man with whom he'd struck up a conversation in a Berlin sex club, of all places. I can't quite imagine how the discussion went, nor am I suggesting that sex clubs are necessarily the ideal place to meet investors, but it shows the power of talking about your ideas whenever (and wherever) you can. This founder went on to run a hugely profitable business, providing networking services to a lot of happy cats!

Early stage equity funding

The main sources of early stage funding are:

- friends and family;
- pre-seed investors, including angel investors and early stage funds; and
- accelerators.

Friends and family

It's not unusual for entrepreneurs to tap up friends and family for help with paying for set-up costs and launching a minimum viable product (MVP). This can help to demonstrate the viability of the business. The amounts are mostly small, although one of our clients raised a cool £1 million from his friends and family. That taught me two things: my friends are a bit rubbish, and my family are not nearly rich enough. But such is life.

Pre-seed investors

Once you're up and running on a basic level you can do a pre-seed funding round, raising anything between £50,000 and £500,000 in return for equity. In fact, some of our clients comfortably raise up to £1 million – it depends on the business, its growth profile, and the valuation that they're able to achieve. I suggest that you don't want to give away too much equity at this stage – between 10 and 20 percent is ideal.

Who are 'pre-seed' investors? They're primarily angel investors or early stage funds. Angel investors are relatively high net worth individuals who look for two things in a start-up:

- a viable business that will scale and return to them a multiple of their investment on exit (or maybe a solid dividend over time, if it's a lifestyle business); and
- assuming they're based in the UK, tax relief on their investment, as the government grants generous tax rebates to certain types of investors in start-ups.

To attract investment from an angel you need to make sure that you have a potentially successful business, with a business plan and pitch deck to prove it. You should also be able to show that you've worked out your financials and that your start-up has legs, so that investors can feel confident about exiting within a reasonable time frame.

What about early stage funds? These are either:

- groups of angel investors working together;
- investment funds which source and manage investments on behalf of other investors; or
- feeder funds for large venture capital firms (VCs).

To attract investment from an early stage fund you'll need similar credentials to the ones that angels are looking for, but be aware that there are some potential downsides to taking investment from this source. Here's a comparison of angels versus early stage funds.

Valuations

Because early stage funds have obligations to their own investors to negotiate hard for a good deal, they tend to give lower valuations than angels. They also push for larger option pools (see Chapter 8 for why that might be a bad thing for you). Both of these factors can have negative consequences for the long-term value and growth of your business.

Control

Early stage funds usually demand more control over your business than do angels. Investors of all types are minority shareholders, so they don't have an automatic right to a say in how you run your company. Angels are usually okay with this, being satisfied with non-voting board observer rights at most, but funds will almost always insist on the right to appoint a director. As a business owner, you need to ensure that you and your co-founders hold the majority of votes at each board meeting. When you give directorships to investors, it may result in you losing that majority.

All investors (whether angel or early stage funds) ask for a list of veto rights to ensure that they have the ability to block the most important decisions you take as a business, such as changing the articles, issuing further shares, removing directors, or winding up the company. Angels usually request a relatively short list of vetos which focus only on their key areas of concern, whereas funds demand a list that can run to several pages. Ask yourself if you want to give up this amount of control.

Fees

Early stage funds charge more (and higher) fees than do angels, which means that you'll be diverting valuable budgets that you could use elsewhere. Many charge not only an upfront fee when they complete the deal, but also ongoing annual fees to compensate them for their time spent keeping an eye on your business, and for their appointed director. They usually set these fees to continue until you exit, so you should always try to put a time limit on them.

Added value

Early stage funds rarely open doors and add value to start-ups in the way that later stage VCs can do. Some have great advisors working for them, but you can buy that kind of advice from elsewhere if you need to – it would certainly be better value when you take into account the fees charged by the funds.

Speed and ease

Given all this, why do business owners choose to work with early stage funds? It's because they tend to invest the money more quickly and easily than angels. Putting together angel rounds can take up a lot of time and energy, and you'll end up with a large number of investors to manage. With funds you only have one person (or a small team) to deal with, and they make fast decisions. Who doesn't like to take the straightforward route now and again?

By this stage you may have a vision of early stage funds being run by ruthless financiers who cackle with delight every time they bag a new victim. However, in my personal experience nothing could be further from the truth – they're actually good people. If you think about it from their point of view, they have obligations to their own investors to make sure that they have the right protections in place should founders go wildly off track. After all, it's other people's money that they're investing. It's also fair to say that most of the early stage fund managers I've met don't ever want to use the protections they insist on – they're only there as a last resort. However, as a business owner you have to assume that if you give away any rights, they'll be exercised.

Accelerators

These are companies that offer a programme of services to make you 'investment ready', such as strategic, marketing, technical, and legal advice. Once you've used these services to give your business a more solid footing, the accelerator will pull together a set of investors for you to pitch to, with a view to you gaining first-round funding. In return, most accelerators take payment in equity and invoice for the services they provide.

Accelerators are popular in the London market, and there are some excellent ones that both deliver high quality services and have a varied and active set of investors for you to pitch to. These accelerators are well connected and can expand your network with useful, start-up centric people. The quality of founders they work with is usually high, so you have the benefit of surrounding yourself with driven and able people. Moreover the investors they put you in front of are credible and genuinely looking for start-ups to invest in. You can find a list of the best accelerators in the market here: www.buckworths.com/accelerators.

Unfortunately, many other accelerators are poor value. They don't provide high quality services, and the investors they introduce are limited in number, which means that you'll be lucky to meet one who happens to be looking to invest in a business like yours right now. The problem with these substandard accelerators is that you have no recourse if they don't deliver what they promise, even though you've given them a chunk of equity. My personal view is that unless you're working with one of the large accelerators such as those in the list on the weblink given in the previous paragraph, or an accelerator that's a specialist in your sector, it rarely makes sense to sign up with one. And if you do, make sure that you check out the businesses they've worked with – speak to as many as you can and try to find out what the accelerator delivered. Most of all, don't be fooled by an accelerator's claims to have helped businesses in the past that are now well-known – it may be that they were just lucky enough to work with a company that later became a household name.

Later stage equity funding

You may carry out one or more pre-seed rounds, but at some point you'll probably reach the stage at which you need a significant cash injection to scale your business. Maybe you want to go from £100,000 of revenue to £10 million, or to expand globally. This is when you look to VCs to raise what's known as a 'Series A' funding round, raising between around £2 million to £50 million in investment (your next investment round would be 'Series B').

VCs are professional, managed investment funds. Often backed by government money, they're made up of high net worth angels and sometimes corporate investors. Most VCs have strict rules on the balance of their investments, the sectors they invest in, and the amount of wriggle room they offer companies with their commercial terms. They invest large chunks of money, but it comes with strings attached. They'll want to exit at a pre-determined multiple of their investment (which is often ten times what they paid in), they'll exercise a lot of control over how you run your business, and they'll want a bunch of economic protections, such as the right to get their money out first in preference to anyone else. However, for many start-ups this is the only route to serious growth.

Your investment journey

There's a traditional fundraising journey that goes from friends and family, to pre-seed investment, to VCs. However, not all start-ups follow the same path. Some companies skip the early stage rounds and raise funds with mainstream VCs from the beginning. Others raise all the funds they need through a series of angel rounds. Nor do the names that people call funding rounds have much meaning, at least in the UK. For instance, I have a client who's currently in a 'pre-seed' round raising £2 million from a VC.

It's worth bearing in mind that there's no problem with not raising any investment at all if you don't want to, or with taking on just enough to scale and keeping most of your company for yourself. It depends on what you want to achieve. As long as your investors are on the same page as you in terms of your growth and exit plans (if any), it's up to you.

What's more, there are other ways of raising investment than approaching angels and funds, which we'll look at next.

Crowdfunding

You've probably heard of crowdfunding platforms such as Crowdcube and Seedrs. They work by having a large number of investors signed up to them, who are looking to invest in the start-ups that market themselves on the site. Once the start-ups have met their investment targets their rounds are closed, they issue the shares to their investors, and receive the money.

Or that's the theory. In practice, investors are usually reluctant to engage with a business until they can see others doing the same, so you'll need to have investors in your back pocket whom you've primed to kickstart your campaign. They'll drip feed investment into it, so that there's a continued interest and progress towards your target. You'll have to bring around half the money you want to raise from your own investors, rather than relying wholly on the platform.

You can see how crowdfunding sites aren't really suitable for early stage start-ups, although that's the type of business that's often drawn to them. The most successful campaigns that I've seen are the equivalent of second or third angel rounds. You need to have existing investor relationships, as well as the ability to make the most of the marketing leverage you'll gain. That means having a finessed product range that you can scale rapidly, and the ability to take on lots of new customers straightaway.

These platforms make most sense as a marketing tool, and for that they can be excellent. You can gain exposure to a huge network of investors through their slick marketing machine, and journalists love to publish stories about innovative companies doing well on them. So if you're at the right stage and want to accelerate your growth, they're definitely something to consider. Also, bear in mind that everything is negotiable with crowdfunding platforms, so you should try to minimise their fees if you can.

Loans

What if you don't want to give away equity, but would prefer to take out a business loan instead? There are times when this might be the best option, but first let's look at how equity compares to loans.

Advantages of equity

- You don't have to repay the investment or worry about what will happen if you can't.
- Shareholders have less control over your business than do lenders.

- When your business is sold (or liquidated), shareholders rank equally to one another and may not get their money back, whereas lenders rank above shareholders and receive their money back first.
- Shareholders' holdings are diluted as new shares are issued, so the percentage of your business that they own slowly reduces. However, the amount you owe to lenders remains the same (or may increase with interest) until you pay it off.

Advantages of loans

- Your own shareholding isn't diluted in the way that it is when you give away equity, so you receive more of the business' profits on an ongoing basis, and the proceeds of sale when you exit.

As you can see, the advantages of loans are few whereas those of equity are many, which is why it's almost always better for a start-up to take equity investment rather than a loan. An exception might be if your company is already successful *and* you're confident that you can repay the loan. Suppose you make and sell cereal bars and need a larger factory so that you can expand, knowing that when you have more capacity your turnover will double. You're confident that you can pay off a loan, and by borrowing the money you won't have to give away any of your business. In that kind of scenario, a loan makes better sense than equity.

Outside London, where there's less angel activity than in the capital, loans are more common and many of them come from funds backed by the UK government. They're distributed by companies or debt funds.

Convertible loans

This is a hybrid between a loan and an equity investment. The way it works is that you borrow money from a lender, paying interest on it until the end of the term just as you would with a normal loan. However, you (or the lender) have the option to convert it into equity, giving them shares in your company instead of paying back the money.

Why use convertibles? Because they avoid you having to set a valuation for the investment today. Let's say you've just launched your MVP (minimum viable product) and so far have little traction. Your investors are prepared to invest at a company valuation of £500,000 in return for shares. However, you're sure that with their money you could quickly gain a huge amount of traction and raise your business valuation to £1 million. So you persuade your investors to give you a convertible loan instead, which will convert into shares six months later at a (say) 20 percent discount to the next investment round valuation. This means that your convertible investor will pay 20 percent less per share than the investors in that round.

Your job here is to work out what valuation you hope to achieve in six months' time, to ensure that you're not in a worse position then. There's a risk. If your company value increases above £625,000 you're better off than if you carried out a straight equity round at £500,000 today, but not if it's lower.

Start-up loans

The British Business Bank (the bank that the UK government uses to lend money to businesses) offers start-up loans to founders of up to £25,000. These are personal loans for which the founder remains liable, although the start-up can fund its repayment. Along with the loan, the bank provides a year of free mentoring.

Grants

It's easy to dismiss grants as being only for charities and not-for-profit organisations, but that's not the case. In fact, they represent free cash that's available to many kinds of organisations, and we all like a bit of that, don't we? Innovate UK, the government's innovation funding arm, offers numerous grants for start-ups – you can apply at https://apply-for-innovation-funding.service.gov.uk/competition/search. It's well worth a couple of hours browsing through the site, especially if you have an innovative business. I've seen start-ups gain grants in areas as diverse as fintech, medtech, cryptocurrencies, and automated marketing functionality.

There's also a lot of money available. The government allocated a whopping additional £1.5 billion to the pot for additional support due to the COVID-19 pandemic, and to offset the reduction in grant funding due to Brexit. Many of the grants are generous, although they often require you to raise matched funding. There are also ones offered by the devolved administrations and certain local authorities, such as sums given to start-ups that incorporate in Wales and have a registered office with at least one employee there. We have a couple of clients who've taken advantage of this, and although their main teams are in London they each have a smaller team based in a Cardiff office.

The downside of grants is that they can be time-consuming and painful to apply for. You have to provide reams of information, and will probably have to work with external companies as well. They only make sense if you fall squarely within the rules of the specific grant. The mistake I've seen some people make is to create an artificial project that meets the requirements, but which the competitive application process usually spots and weeds out. Even if they do succeed, they'll only have committed themselves to spending time and energy on something that isn't central to their business, and what's the point of that?

Companies that offer to raise funds for you

The fundraising arena can seem like a bit of a jungle when you first enter it. This has spawned a plethora of companies that claim to be experts in all things business-related, especially when it comes to putting entrepreneurs in touch with investors. But can you trust them?

At the upper end of the market are investment banks that can help you secure tens of millions of pounds of investment. In my experience, they deliver value. However, it won't surprise you to learn that their services come with a huge price tag, with commissions of at least £1m for any investment round that they manage. As such, they're only relevant for businesses already worth at least £50 to 100 million.

At the lower end of the market you have to be far more wary. The last few years have seen numerous outfits pop up that claim to raise investment for start-ups. The way they work is to take some of your equity, charge a monthly retainer, and also slice off a percentage of the funds they raise. At best it's an expensive way for you to gain investment, but the main problem is that these businesses often don't deliver. Not only have you wasted your time, potentially delaying your funding round and even running out of money, but you've given away equity and cash with nothing to show for it.

From talking to many start-ups that have dealt with these intermediaries, here are the warning signs:

- they insist on upfront equity that's not tied to any performance metrics;
- they want a monthly retainer fee for a minimum period; and
- they receive a commission from any investment you gain, even if it's not from people introduced by them, and even if you've terminated your agreement in the meanwhile.

I've learned that it doesn't matter how slick their websites are or how reputable they seem, you should never agree to pay these companies anything that isn't performance related. Also, check that they're FCA authorised, as in most circumstances charging a fee for introducing investors constitutes the regulated activity of 'arranging deals in investments'. If they're not regulated, ask them why.

To me, using these intermediaries is a bit of a lazy way to go about raising funds. If you've made an effort to build up your network you shouldn't need them, because it's not hard to find investors in the London market when you put yourself out there. In fact, you don't even have to be in London – the sky will do. One of our clients had a private jet business that sold 'empty legs' to make money out of planes that would otherwise have been flying without passengers between locations. In the early stages of setting it up he was on a commercial flight to New York and struck up a conversation with the lady next to him. He started waxing lyrical about his start-up, and she suggested some helpful tweaks to his business model. It transpired that she was the founder of a New York VC, which ended up investing many millions in his business and introducing him to a bunch of ultra-high-net-worth people who became his customers. This is a perfect example of how talking to people about your ideas can pay dividends.

Tax reliefs

Fundraising doesn't only have to be about bringing money in, it can also be about paying less out. Once you start trading, it's worth checking what tax reliefs may be available. Research and development (R&D) tax reliefs are generous, giving cash rebates based on how much you spend on research and development. Depending on the stage of your start-up, and how much you invest in this area, these reliefs can run into hundreds of thousands of pounds. Also, if you have a patent you might be able to claim a further tax relief called 'patent box' relief. Tax reliefs are one topic that it's essential to talk to your accountant about, as they're highly complex.

In the next chapter I'll explain how to get the best valuation for your company, as this is the first step towards gaining investment.

The wrap-up

- To win the attention of investors, you need to be networking and talking about your business from day one.
- Early stage funding is made up of a different set of investor types than later stage funding.
- Other sources of funding are crowdfunding, grants, and loans.
- You're best to go direct to sources of funding, rather than to use intermediaries.

Chapter 8

How to value your company

Make your equity go further

Before you embark on raising investment you need to put a value on your company. It's an exciting moment when you see a figure that represents all the hard work you've put in, but coming up with a valuation can also be a difficult thing to do. Different experts say different things, and there's no single correct way to go about it. The way forward is to understand the options, so you can work out what's right for you. In this chapter I'll explain how to calculate your valuation, so you can walk into your first investor meeting with confidence.

You'll learn:

- the basic principles to apply when calculating your valuation;
- the impact that option pools can have on it; and
- various methods of coming up with a valuation.

The basic principles

First, the maths. If you're like many founders, you hate it. That's okay, you don't have to be an expert in numbers – that's what your accountant or finance person is for. But you do need to understand the basics, so you can avoid making rookie mistakes that will cost your business dearly in the future. What follows are the principles to get your head around, so you can build your valuation on rock.

The importance of calculating the right valuation

Setting up a business that raises investment at a high initial valuation is an ego boost for any entrepreneur, but it's important for more reasons than that.

First, the higher the valuation of your company, the less of it you'll need to give away in equity to investors. For instance, if your business is valued at £800,000 and you gain £200,000 of investment, the investors will receive 20 percent of your shares in return. But if the valuation is £1.8 million and you gain the same amount of investment, the investors receive only ten percent. You've secured the same sum of money, but have given away less of the voting rights, rights to profit, and share of sale. (If these figures don't seem correct to you, you've made the same mistake as most people, so please read on.)

Second, having a high valuation helps when you eventually come to exit. There are a number of different models used to value a business at sale, but by default the purchaser will look back at your previous investment round valuations, especially if they're relatively recent. Imagine that you want to sell your company for £50 million, but a year ago you carried out an investment round at which it was valued at £5 million. That's going to be a challenging conversation for you to have with a buyer. But if you can show that you raised your first round at

£3 million, then £10 million, and finally at £25 million, it's an easier story to tell.

That said, it's a mistake to raise a round at an implausibly high valuation. Why? Because you could end up having to carry out your next round at a lower one, which can be extremely problematic (more detail on this later).

Pre- and post-money valuations

It's helpful to know a couple of key terms at this point. The first is 'pre-money valuation': that's the value of your company today, before you gain any investment. When we talk about 'valuation', we mean the pre-money. The second is 'post-money valuation': that's the value of your company after your investment round is complete.

Post-money valuation = pre-money valuation + total amount of investment in the round.

For example, if the pre-money valuation of your company is £800,000 and you raise £200,000 of investment, the post-money valuation is £1 million.

Working out share percentages and price per share

That might seem obvious, but it's the first step to avoiding the *number one investment mistake* that entrepreneurs make, which is to give away a larger percentage of equity than they need to by calculating the investor's percentage incorrectly. Many founders divide the amount being invested by the *pre-*

money valuation. This is wrong! It should be the *post-money* valuation, as the following correct formula shows:

*Investor's percentage = investment amount / **post-money** valuation.*

The reason for using the post-money valuation is that when an investor invests, you always issue *new* shares. Therefore the total number of shares increases. The percentage that the investor holds is the percentage of the new, increased amount of shares that your company is now made up of. In our example, your investors are putting in £200,000 at a post-money valuation of £1 million, so they receive 20 percent of the company's shares. Had you incorrectly used the pre-money valuation of £800,000, the investors would have received 25 percent.

So that's the investors' percentage explained, but how do you calculate the price per share that they'll pay? Here's the formula:

Price per share = pre-money valuation / total number of shares in the fully diluted share capital.

Hang on, why are we using the pre-money valuation when I've just explained why your post-money valuation is what your investors' share percentages should be based on? Because unlike the share percentage, the share price is based on the valuation of the company *before* any investment is made. Returning to our example, imagine that prior to investment there were 10,000 shares in your fully diluted share capital (I'll explain what 'fully diluted share capital' means in a moment – for now, just think of it as being the total number of shares in your business). Applying the formula in the example's case, the price per share would be £800,000 / 10,000 = £80 per share.

We can check this is correct by looking at it from a different angle. The investment of £200,000, divided by a price per share of £80, comes to 2,500 new shares to be issued to the investors. That means that the *new* total number of shares will be 12,500. The investors' shares (2,500) divided by the new total number of shares (12,500) works out at 20 percent. This matches the calculation we did earlier.

Diluted share capital explained

I mentioned 'fully diluted share capital' earlier, and it's important to understand what this means. There are two cap tables that exist for most start-ups:

- **The issued cap table:** this is the record of shares that have been issued and are held by shareholders.
- **The fully diluted cap table:** this is the total number of issued shares above, plus any shares that have been promised to be issued in the future, including options. As you'll remember from Chapter 4, options are rights to acquire shares in the future if certain conditions are met. They're classed as being 'reserved' in the 'option pool' in the fully diluted cap table, with the shares only being issued and recorded at Companies House if an option holder exercises their option and acquires the shares.

Investors usually invest on the basis of the fully diluted cap table, *not* the issued cap table. That's because there's always the potential for options to be exercised, which would have the effect of diluting their percentage. This is why, when you calculate the price per share that they'll pay, you have to imagine that all the options (and other rights to acquire shares) have been fully issued. To do this, you include any shares that could be issued as part of the pre-investment share capital.

The effect of option pools on your valuation

Because option pools are included in the pre-investment cap table, they have the effect of reducing the effective valuation of your company. However, although investors invest on the basis that all shares in the option pool will be issued, in most cases that never happens. On exit unused options simply vanish, so that each shareholder's portion of the sale proceeds increases.

In our example, pre-investment, your fully diluted share capital was 10,000 shares. Assume that of those 10,000 shares, 9,000 shares were issued and 1,000 were reserved as an option pool. Your pre-investment cap table would look like this:

9,000 issued shares
1,000 reserved as an option pool

Post-investment, your fully diluted cap table would look like this:

11,500 issued shares (as you issued 2,500 new shares to investors)
1,000 reserved as an option pool

Now let's imagine that your start-up does extremely well and is sold. You haven't needed to raise any investment on top of the £200,000 that you've already taken, and for which you gave away 2,500 shares. What's more, none of the option pool is used up, as any employees who were granted options have left the business without exercising them and receiving their shares.

When your business is sold, the purchaser buys all of the issued shares. If there'd been options outstanding and capable of exercise, those would have become issued shares at that point. However, none of the options were exercised so the option pool disappears. The purchaser therefore buys the following shares:

9,000 issued shares held by the founders
2,500 issued shares held by the investors
0 shares in the options pool

You'll remember that your investors received 20 percent of the fully diluted share capital when they invested. When you consider that the total number of shares sold to the purchaser is 11,500, this means that the investors receive 21.74 percent of the sale proceeds and *not* the 20 percent they would have done if there had never been an option pool. The effective valuation at which the investors invested was therefore not £800,000, but £720,000.

What does this mean to you? That the bigger your option pool, the lower the effective valuation of your company. This is why, when an investor pushes you to create a larger option pool, they're not necessarily concerned about your ability to incentivise future employees. Rather, they may be trying to reduce the effective valuation so that they can gain a larger percentage of your company for the same money (banking on many of the options not being exercised). They may say something like, 'We'll invest £200,000, but we think there should be an option pool of ten percent. That's because you'll need to recruit experienced people and incentivise them with options.' This may be sound business advice, but it's far from impartial.

As a founder, you'll want to keep your option pool as small as possible so as to maximise the effective valuation of your company, while at the same time retaining the ability to grant options as needed. You can always decide to increase your option pool in the future – you'll probably do it at each investment round in any case. Just don't be fooled into agreeing to a large option pool on your first round.

I've put together a helpful tool for you to calculate your cap table and the impact of increasing the size of your option pool here: www.buckworths.com/captablecalculator

Coming up with a valuation

There are many ways of calculating a valuation for your start-up. Deciding which is the most applicable to you will depend on the type of investor you're dealing with and the stage your business is at. For instance, a common way to value a business that's been trading for a few years is to apply a multiple to earnings. These are often in the range of 5x to 8x for many tech businesses, and 8x to 12x – or sometimes significantly higher – for SaaS businesses. However, if your start-up isn't yet trading in any significant way, or is still at seed or early growth stage, it would have a value of £0 if you used this method. That's why pre-revenue start-ups tend to use one or a combination of the following approaches instead.

Discounted cash flow

With this, you estimate the total market for your product or service. Then you forecast how much you'll grow your market share between launch and a specified time in the future, along with the cash flow to fund fixed and variable costs, future working capital, and capital expenditure. After that you apply a discount rate to your forecasts, which is designed to take account of the risk inherent in a start-up. The earlier the stage of your business, the larger the discount will be. This is the method that's most common for investors to use, which is why having coherent and well-thought-through financial forecasts is vital.

Comparison with other start-ups

It's important that you know at what valuations other start-ups in your sector have raised investment, and how they're now valued. You want to drill down into the numbers behind the valuations as much as you can. All UK companies have to publish a return (a form SH01) at Companies House every time they issue shares. This shows the number of shares issued, along with the price paid per share – you can figure out the approximate valuation (ignoring any option pool) from that information. There's no better way to defend your assumptions than to point to other start-ups in your space which have raised investment at your valuation, and gone on to be successful.

Customer value

For some businesses it's possible to put a value on each customer acquisition. This tends to work better for later stage companies, but can sometimes be a good method for start-ups close to (or soon after) launch. The idea is that you calculate a value per customer based on how long they'll stay with you and what they'll spend. You then combine this with a forecast of your customer acquisition numbers (taking into account any attrition) to come to a valuation.

Dilution

This isn't very scientific, but many founders calculate a valuation by working backwards from the percentage of equity that they want to hold post-investment. For instance, if you're raising £1 million and you want to give your investors a maximum of 20 percent, your pre-money valuation needs to be £4 million or more. That might seem more like wish fulfilment than science, but it's a surprisingly common approach. It helps you to figure out what you want your valuation to be, and enables you to structure a cash flow forecast that predicts how much revenue your business needs to be turning over by a certain point in the future.

In a way, the dilution method is an admission of the subjective nature of the valuation process for start-ups that are yet to see much trading. Investors are usually interested in the person as much as the business, and attribute value to the company based on where they think it may be able to go in the future. That said, if you use this model you need to consider others as well.

An important note on valuations

It can be tempting to try to push your valuation as high as you possibly can, but please resist this. If you end up securing a sky-high valuation for your first round you may find it impossible to match it in subsequent rounds, especially if you haven't met your revenue and customer acquisition targets. That would force you to do what's called a 'down round', in which you try to raise funds at a lower valuation – something that brings considerable risk. If in doubt, raise at a realistic valuation, deliver on your targets, and hike your valuation in the next round.

One of our clients, which operates a loyalty scheme for a niche sector, managed to raise £1.5 million at a staggering pre-money valuation of £30 million for its first round. It was based on the fact that in the area in which it operates, the company would only need to win two or three key customers to lead to mass adoption of its services across the sector. However, for a number of unforeseeable reasons, including the COVID-19 pandemic, the founders only managed to sign up one client before needing to raise more money in a second round. Subsequent investors refused to invest at the original valuation, so our client had to settle for raising £2 million at a £4 million pre-money valuation. Its initial valuation had been far too aggressive, and the company paid for it. Had the founders raised their first round at a valuation of £5 to £7 million (which would still have been punchy) they could have sold the success story of their first client, and raised their next round at a higher one. Setting your valuation should not always be about how much you think you can get away with.

In the London market, if you want to raise more than £100,000 you ought to target a valuation of at least £1 million. In fact most tech, SaaS, and high-growth businesses raise their first round at more. The majority of our clients, especially those in the SaaS space, routinely raise successful first rounds at pre-money valuations of £2 to £4 million. However, if your business isn't scalable, is very high risk, or perhaps isn't as exciting as others, you may end up raising at a lower level.

In the next chapter we'll look at the pros and cons of raising investment over different timescales, so you can gain the best value from the funds that you bring in.

The wrap-up

- Make sure that you understand the basic principles of calculating a company valuation if you want to avoid costing yourself money in the long-term.
- There are various ways for start-ups to value themselves, and it may be a combination of them that's right for you.
- Don't value your business too highly unless you're sure that you can deliver on your performance milestones.

How's Lucio doing?

Lucio knows that this is crunch time: he needs to raise a significant first investment round to pay for the developers who'll create his platform. His CTO will be heavily involved, but Peter can't do it all on his own. In addition, Lucio wants funds to cover his launch and other marketing activities.

Using the dilution method, he calculates that £1 million seems like a sensible amount to raise, but he doesn't want to give away more than 15 percent of his equity, which means that his pre-money valuation has to be £5,666,000:

Pre-money valuation of £5,666,000 + investment of £1,000,000 = post-money valuation of £6,666,000.

The percentage of shares that his investors will receive is: £1,000,000 / £6,666,000 = 15 percent.

Lucio has never seen figures as being his strong point, but with the help of his accountant he grits his teeth and creates cash flow and profit and loss forecasts. He also compares his business to a number of his competitors.

After he's done this, he takes a fresh look at his numbers. It occurs to him that to justify the valuation he has to predict sky-high client acquisition and revenue numbers, and he doesn't think these are achievable. Rather than risk missing his predictions and ending up having to carry out a down round, he decides that his best option is to reduce the amount he'll raise to £750,000 and his valuation to £3 million.

Pre-money valuation of £3,000,000 + investment of £750,000 = post-money valuation of £3,750,000.

The percentage of shares that his investors will receive is £750,000 / £3,750,000 = 20 percent.

He feels that this is more realistic, and similar to where his competitors were at when they carried out their first rounds. What's more, the various conversations he's been having with angels confirm his instincts, which reassures him that he's in the right ballpark.

Lucio has been hitting the investment networking circuit hard, and has found it useful to gain feedback on his idea as well as to build relationships with angel investors. In an attempt to cover all bases he also speaks with a couple of impressive-looking early stage funds, but they push back on his valuation and want a ten percent option pool.

In the end, he decides to carry out the whole round with a group of angels. One invests £200,000, and introduces him to his friends, who between them invest a further £350,000. This is a fantastic result for Lucio. With such a great start, he's confident he can raise the remaining £200,000 without much difficulty, and sets up some investor calls to close out the final tranche.

For the first time, Pre-Train is starting to look like it will definitely happen – it's an amazing moment. His next phone call home will be very different to the previous conversations, in which he's tried to convince his extended family that he hasn't lost his mind by setting up a new business. Now he's the proud owner of a company worth nearly £4 million. That's something to celebrate.

Chapter 9

When to raise funds

Get your timing right

You know where to find investment and how to value your company, but what should you do next? Would it be best to raise all the funds in one go, or to spread them out? And do you even need to raise any funds at all – maybe there's an alternative? There's more to think about than you might imagine, which is why we'll explore the options when it comes to the timing of investment. You'll learn:

- whether or not to raise funds before launch;
- the pros and cons of carrying out large versus small investment rounds;
- whether to have one closing or multiple closings; and
- whether trading equity for services makes sense.

To raise or not to raise?

There's nothing to say that you have to raise investment before you launch your start-up. Some founders bootstrap their businesses and try to delay a first investment round for as long as possible. This is often out of desire to be self-sufficient, and also to retain their full equity so that they can keep all their profits and proceeds of sale. There's also the rationale that the further a company is on its growth trajectory, the higher its valuation will be when it comes to approaching investors – why not give it time to climb? In many cases this is a sensible approach, but you need to be aware of the risks.

Standing out isn't always helpful

Imagine you're going for a job interview at a corporate business – not likely now that you're an entrepreneur, I realise, but you can use your imagination. Would you turn up in a fluorescent pink onesie, or even an outrageously expensive outfit that looks a bit out of place? I don't think so. You'd want to appear predictable, professional, and as if you already work there. You'd let your skills and experience do the talking, not your wacky dress sense.

In the same way, taking an unusual route to investment can be a disadvantage. Of course your business is unique, but VCs looking to invest in a start-up's Series A round usually expect to see a company that's raised money before and has shown that it can spend it wisely. One that's been bootstrapped from the start, but is now seeking a £5 million cash injection at its first round, might struggle to attract the right investors because it appears to be higher risk. This isn't a hard and fast rule – I have some clients who've raised a Series A round in this way. But I know many more who've struggled to pull it off.

Even with angels, who tend to invest on a more varied and personal basis, there's a broad expectation about what valuation a first round should be at. If you focus first on putting your MVP out there with the hopes that it will skyrocket your valuation, you'll probably be disappointed. There's often a minimal difference in value between a start-up raising investment with only a business plan and a team of founders, and one that's added an MVP into the mix. Low marketing budgets usually result in poor traction, and a company with few sales isn't worth much more than one with none. Even worse, you could launch your MVP and run out of money before achieving investment, which would send your valuation even lower than it would have been if you'd raised earlier. In the worst case scenario you could find yourself falling between two stools: too long in the tooth for an angel (who may want to claim tax reliefs which are only applicable when investing in young start-ups), and with too little traction for a VC.

Large or small round?

Suppose you want £500,000 to launch your business, and plan to spend it over 12 months. You need £100,000 to start off with and the rest could come later if necessary. Should you raise an initial £100,000 and then carry out a £400,000 round when needed, or raise the full amount in one go? This is a common dilemma, so let's look at the factors to consider.

Time and energy

I firmly believe that you need to view fundraising as an ongoing activity, especially in the early stages. You should see every conversation as potentially leading to investment, and build each investor who expresses an interest into your investment funnel while you nurture the relationship. Of course, this absorbs time and energy that you could be using in other ways to build your business. That's why it's sometimes worth closing a round with as much funding as you can, rather than delaying or raising one smaller round after another.

Another reason for doing it this way is that a bird (or in this case, an investor) in the hand is worth three in the bush. Many start-ups fail not because their business idea is a bad one, but because they misjudge when they need to raise money or are caught out by events (the Brexit referendum and COVID-19 being classic recent examples). There are times when closing a larger round today, perhaps at a lower valuation than you might have achieved later, is better than the possibility of a round tomorrow. To give you a brutal example, back in 2016 one of our clients sought to raise £1 million from angels at a pre-money valuation of £4.5 million. The round was oversubscribed, with interest from £2 million of angels. The business was outperforming its targets and wasn't set to run out of money for a couple of months, so the founders felt that the valuation could shoot higher if they waited a bit. As it happened, the business did extremely well and they returned to investors to raise their round. The problem was that in the meantime the Brexit referendum had taken place, causing the investment market to plunge into a six-month deep freeze. The company ended up going bust because it ran out of cash.

That said, there's a potential downside to raising more money than you need right now. One of our clients aimed to raise £750,000, and managed to secure £2 million. They took the money because they didn't want to spend time raising a further round, but the problem was that their company valuation was lower than if they'd waited – £2 million of investment represented a huge dilution in shares. In my view they'd have been better off taking a maximum of £1 million, letting the business grow, boosting its valuation, and raising the rest later.

Investor expectations

Early stage investors often have expectations about the percentages they want to receive, which might not be that different whether they're investing £20,000 or £100,000. This means that you might be substantially worse off if you carry out a larger number of small rounds than a smaller number of large rounds.

Whether to raise a large or small round is a difficult question to answer and you may not get it right. This is a natural part of doing business. You'll make good decisions and you'll make bad ones – the trick is to accept that you'll make some misjudgements and will learn from them.

Also, as an aside, it's much better to focus on your company's valuation than the share percentage when talking to investors. Sometimes start-ups are so fixated on not giving away one more percent that they let a deal go, when that percent would be significantly diluted by the time they'd carried out three more investment rounds. It's easy to lose sight of the big picture.

One closing or multiple closings?

Ten years ago, defined rounds were the norm. As soon as the money was in your account and the investment documentation complete, the round would close. Then you'd go away, grow your business, and return to raise another round a year or so later. After the Brexit referendum this all changed, and start-ups had to take money where they could find it. If a business owner landed a £50,000 investor they'd thank their lucky stars, issue the shares, and carry on raising investment elsewhere. To a certain extent this more flexible approach has carried on, so although there's nothing wrong with doing a fixed round, if it's taking longer than you'd like you can often choose to close it out in tranches.

Another advantage of doing it this way is that you can sometimes increase your company's valuation within a round. Once you start spending your investment money you're potentially generating increased traction and revenue, which means that you can justify a slightly higher valuation for the next tranche. So you can take some of the money, pause your round, increase your valuation, and take an investment at a higher valuation for the rest. After all, your business has grown and so later investors are taking less risk.

However, investors may only be prepared to invest if you reach a certain threshold of investment within a round. If your pitch deck says that you need £100,000 to launch, investors may not be prepared to release their funds if you've only raised £50,000 so far. Will you be successful in finding the remainder?

As a final note, always remember that there's an added compliance cost if you issue shares on separate days. This is especially the case if your investors are claiming tax relief on their investments. A helpful way of keeping costs down is to issue shares on as few days as possible, even if you're closing a round in tranches.

Cash or equity for services?

I often see businesses which, in an understandable attempt to keep their costs low, engage suppliers whom they pay in equity rather than cash. I've seen it go hideously wrong far more often than it goes right.

When start-ups pay a service provider with cash, it's normal to keep an eye on their performance. Hopefully they only pay a proportion of the fees up front, and set milestones for delivery before they pay the rest. If they're not happy, they cancel the contract. But when start-ups pay in equity, for some reason they don't follow the same process. Often they agree milestones with equity attached to them, but not in the same level of detail, and nor do they monitor the progress as carefully. It seems that when it's cash they care, but when it's equity they don't see it as having the same value.

Also, think about it from the perspective of the service provider who's being paid in equity. They won't see the financial payback on their work for many months or years to come, and there's no guarantee that it will even materialise then. So when a cash-paying client comes along and demands their time and energy in preference to the one paying in equity, who will they favour?

For this reason, among others, these relationships often fail. In the worst cases they end up in court, and even then the entrepreneur is unlikely to receive substantial compensation for work that wasn't satisfactorily done. They might want all or some of their equity to be returned. However, it's rare for a judge to award this, partly because of the impact it could have on their other shareholders, and also because courts tend not to force people to transfer assets. Instead, the business owner will probably receive a cash sum linked to the value of their company's shares today, which may be lower than the value of the services. So £100,000 given away in equity for £100,000 of work that wasn't completed on time, might turn into a £5,000 cash refund. Not only that, but they're saddled with a shareholder with whom they've fallen out and who has a permanent chunk of equity in their business. All in all, it's better to raise cash through investment and use that to pay your service providers on standard commercial terms, than it is to pay them with equity.

In the next chapter we'll explore the impact that investor tax reliefs have on how you pitch to investors, so that you can make sure your company is as attractive for investment as possible.

The wrap-up

- There's a lot more flexibility than you might think when it comes to the timing and nature of your investment rounds.
- However, deviating from the norm carries some risks.
- It's best to pay with cash rather than equity for business services.

How's Lucio doing?

Lucio's success in raising investment is going from good to great. He ends up attracting investors wanting to put in a grand total of £1.5 million. However, he decides that he doesn't want to take the extra dilution, so he sticks with accepting the £750,000 he originally aimed at.

Despite this, he plans to keep in touch with the investors he turned down. He'll also keep an eye on what happens in the investment market, and if he thinks that he may struggle to raise his next round he might tap up those investors for more money at his initial valuation.

Chapter 10

Making your business attractive to investors

Understand investor tax reliefs

Yes, this chapter is about tax reliefs, and not even your own. Don't groan! I promise that when you've read it you'll see why they're so important to know about. This is why: as I mentioned previously, there are two reasons why UK angel investors (and some VCs) might want to buy into your business. One is the prospect of selling their shares for a healthy profit in the future – in other words, making money from your success. The other is the enormous amount of tax relief that they'll secure in the process.

The UK government offers hugely generous tax breaks to people who invest in start-ups. The idea is that by encouraging them to support your business growth with their money, you're better able to create jobs and boost the national economy. The tax reliefs make a significant difference to how willing investors are to take risks. In an average year, my law firm advises on around 80 investment rounds, of which three quarters include investment from angels looking to claim tax reliefs. In most cases, the investors wouldn't have invested at all otherwise.

This is great news for you, but these tax schemes can be complex and investors expect you to have sorted out the analysis and compliance to ensure that their investment qualifies. So to attract this tax-incentivised investment to your own company, you have to understand what the tax reliefs are and how they work. It's only then that you can make yourself investor-friendly from a tax perspective.

You might assume that angels and VCs know the tax schemes inside out, so why do you need to understand them? In reality, investors tend to have a minimal understanding of the detail – you'd be amazed at how little angels know about this stuff. You might find yourself on the receiving end of questions. You can always ask your solicitor for their advice, but how much more impressive would it be if you could answer them yourself? Your job is to make your potential investors' lives easy so that they say 'yes' to investing in you.

This chapter will cover:

- what the schemes are;
- how to find out if you qualify;
- how to present your business to potential investors in a tax-friendly way; and
- how to avoid invalidating tax reliefs and causing problems with HMRC.

What are the tax-relief schemes?

The two main early stage tax-relief schemes are the Seed Enterprise Investment Scheme (SEIS) and the Enterprise Investment Scheme (EIS). These reduce the risk for investors in high-risk start-ups, by giving them back a percentage of their investment as a credit against their income tax liabilities. They also allow investors a tax-free exit.

It can be helpful to understand how the schemes came about. Back in 1994 the then Prime Minister, John Major, was keen to kickstart the UK economy after a recession. So Kenneth Clarke, his new Chancellor, announced the abolition of the ineffective Business Expansion Scheme and replaced it with EIS. The new scheme was designed to encourage high net worth individuals to make risky investments in start-ups. This would give start-ups a source of funding, which would allow them to recruit staff and grow their businesses, thereby reducing unemployment. In 2012 Chancellor George Osbourne introduced SEIS, a more generous but smaller scheme designed for pre-seed stage companies. SEIS and EIS worked like a dream, and 25 years later London is one of the largest start-up hubs in the world.

SEIS

Let's start with SEIS, which is the scheme that's most immediately relevant to you as an early stage start-up. You could think of it as the 'baby scheme', although the tax reliefs are far from small. SEIS applies to the first £250,000 that angel investors claiming tax relief put into your business. It has a lifetime limit per company, so after one or more investors have used it up, no other investor can take advantage of it when they invest in your start-up. Also, an SEIS investor must make their investment within three years of you beginning to trade, and each investor has a personal SEIS allowance of

£200,000 per tax year which applies across all of their SEIS investments.

There are three tax advantages for investors under SEIS:

- Personal income tax relief equal to up to 50 percent of what the investor invests. So if an individual puts £100,000 into your company, they can claim a reduction of up to £50,000 from their income tax in the tax year that they make the investment (and/or the preceding tax year).

- A deferral of 50 percent of capital gains tax liabilities on the sale of their other investment assets during the tax year. So, if an angel sells an asset (such as a rental property or shares in a listed company), and in the same tax year invests the gain they make in a start-up under SEIS, they only pay half the capital gains tax that they would otherwise have paid on that sale.

- The big one: 100 percent capital gains tax relief when they sell their shares – so they pay no tax whatsoever at that point (subject to the investor and the company complying with a number of detailed rules). A client company of ours was sold to a large tech business for £125 million. One of the investors in that company had originally put in £420,000 under a mix of SEIS and EIS, and sold his shares for a cool £26 million *completely tax free*. Unbelievably to me, many investors don't seem to think much about this amazing benefit, preferring to focus on the upfront income tax relief.

Let's look at the benefits of SEIS through an example. I'm an investor, and I invest £100,000 in a start-up under SEIS. As long as I've paid at least £50,000 worth of UK income tax in the tax year that I make my investment (or the preceding one), I can reclaim up to £50,000 from HMRC. So I've invested £100,000 and received back £50,000 in tax relief, which means that I've only taken £50,000 of risk.

There's more. I've sold shares in a listed company during the same tax year at a profit of £80,000. I'd usually have to pay 20 percent capital gains tax on that (£16,000), as I happen to have used up my capital gains tax allowance for the year. However, if I invest that gain in a start-up under SEIS, I only have to pay half of this: £8,000 (this is called 'deferral relief'). Here's how my tax relief is now working out:

Money invested: £100,000

Tax relief gained: £58,000

Risk I'm taking in making the investment: £42,000

Under the rules of SEIS, I have to hold the shares in the start-up for three years. When I come to sell them, the company has increased in value and my shares are now worth £20 million. I pay no tax whatsoever on the gain I've made – my exit is 100 percent tax free.

If you think that this is a particularly tasty cake for investors already, there's some additional icing. Under both SEIS and EIS, there's also 'downside protection' for the investor. If a start-up goes bust, or if its investors lose their money in some other way, they may be entitled to loss relief. This is complex to calculate so I won't go into it here, but it goes some way towards compensating investors for any losses they make.

EIS

EIS works in much the same way, but rather than being limited to £250,000 of investment it applies to the next £10–12 million (the threshold increases for highly innovative 'knowledge intensive companies' – ones that involve substantial amounts of research and development). In terms of the tax reliefs, the headline differences for EIS are that the investor income tax relief is 30 percent rather than 50 percent, and the deferral tax relief when the investor re-invests a capital gain doesn't apply. Also, the investment must take place within seven years of the company starting to trade, rather than two years (this can be extended if the business is knowledge intensive).

You could think of EIS as the 'grown-up scheme', and while many entrepreneurs focus on SEIS because of the more generous tax reliefs, the big numbers – for the company at least – are in EIS. In reality, the majority of start-ups gain investment from investors using a mixture of SEIS and EIS for their first investment round.

Does your start-up qualify for SEIS and EIS investment?

You may be feeling a bit more interested in these tax-relief schemes by now, but does your business qualify? There are strict rules about this, some of which apply when you gain investment, and others which are more relevant in the future. Be warned: you can retrospectively invalidate your investors' tax reliefs if you don't keep to them.

You must be carrying on a 'qualifying trade'

What constitutes a qualifying trade? It's easier to explain what isn't covered, rather than what is. The main trades that don't qualify include property development and property rental (for instance, the provision of serviced offices). Also not covered are businesses whose revenue mainly comes from hiring out items, such as car rental firms. Having said that, if you're a platform business that matches people who have assets with people who want to hire them, like Uber or Airbnb, you ought to qualify. In this case you're a technology business, because your customers (not you) are renting out the assets.

For instance, we had a client who ran 'dark kitchens', which are warehouses with kitchens used by takeaway restaurants to cook food. The operating model was that restaurants would rent their kitchens by the hour or day, which meant that the company didn't qualify for investor tax relief as it was based on renting out property. However, we had another client who also owned dark kitchens but in this case operated them as part of an accelerator. As well as providing their clients with space in their kitchens, they also taught them how to run successful takeaway businesses. The use of the kitchens was just one part of a broader package of services, and this allowed the company to qualify for the schemes.

Your business must only be worth a certain amount

For SEIS your company's gross asset value (which, by the way, isn't the same thing as its valuation) can't be higher than

£350,000 at the point when you issue shares to your investors. For this reason, you need to check that your accountant hasn't capitalised your expenditure on IP development, and so created assets that make your company worth more. The rule also has critical implications for the timing of receiving your investment money and issuing shares in return, which we'll go into in the next chapter. For EIS there's a much higher gross asset limit of £15,000,000 (which might be a nice problem to have when the time comes).

You must own your intellectual property

To qualify for SEIS or EIS investment, your start-up must own all (or substantially all) of its IP, and that IP must have been created by, or on behalf of, your company. If you've bought IP from elsewhere, you may not qualify. The rules around this are complex, so if you think you may fall foul of them it's best to talk to a solicitor. There's probably a way to make it work, but you need specialist advice.

A common suggestion made by some start-up business advisers is to hold IP in a company owned by the founders, and to licence it to a separate company that will carry on the trade (and in which the investors will invest). The idea behind this is to protect the IP if the trading company goes bust. Some founders go even further and use it as a way of extracting value from the trading company in priority to their investors, by charging a licence fee. This is great in theory and could work well. However, that kind of structure doesn't qualify for SEIS or EIS, and it may not be easy or possible to move the IP and trading into the same entity retrospectively.

As always, it's good to gather a range of views about your business idea and how to make it happen, but you should run people's advice past a solicitor to make sure that there are no unintended consequences.

Your investors' capital must be at risk

SEIS and EIS are extremely generous tax schemes, and for obvious reasons HMRC doesn't want to fling money around in the form of tax breaks when the risk of an investor losing their money is low. If there's little risk, why give the tax relief at all? Most start-ups in the early stages constitute high-risk businesses, so that shouldn't be a problem for you. However, take care not to do what I've seen some founders do, which is to make their businesses appear to be a 'sure bet' by positioning them to investors as low risk. This might make sense in a pitch situation, but you need to give HMRC the same information as your investors. You can't tell HMRC that your start-up is high risk and investors that it's low risk.

That's why it's best to be realistic with your numbers, and to be sure that you can back them up. If you say that your business will explode and achieve £100 million profitability in a year, you may not appear credible. Quite apart from the fact that any sensible investor would run a mile, there's also an argument that their capital is not sufficiently at risk to qualify for tax relief.

A similar problem can arise if your cash flow forecast illustrates that not all of the investment is needed. Suppose you're raising £500,000 and your forecast only allocates £400,000 to specific activities, leaving £100,000 as a contingency. To HMRC that £100,000 is not at risk, and would invalidate your investors' eligibility for tax relief.

You must predict and achieve organic growth

While for both schemes the level of risk is an important factor to HMRC, with EIS the potential for growth is also key. You have to show that the money you seek will lead to the organic growth of employees, revenue, and customer numbers. That's because HMRC doesn't want to subsidise investment in businesses that aren't going to use the money to grow, but are only going to use it to fund working capital or to stay afloat.

However, you shouldn't forecast unrealistic levels of growth – neither HMRC nor investors will be impressed by this. What's more, if you don't end up meeting your crazy forecasts and decide to carry out another investment round in the future, HMRC may say that you don't meet the growth requirement because your performance has come nowhere near your predictions. In the worst case scenario, it might even void the tax relief from your initial investment and claw it back from your investors, especially if it can see that you didn't use all of your investment money to achieve growth. As you can imagine, your investors will be deeply unhappy about this.

You must plan to spend your investment on the right things

There are more restrictions relating to this than I can explain here, but as an example, you can't spend SEIS or EIS money on buying another business. There are circumstances when you can do this using other sources of funding, but if that business started trading on an earlier date than your start-up, your commencement of trading date will be re-set to the earlier date. This effectively voids the period during which your start-up is eligible to raise investment using the schemes.

Your company must have a base in the UK

These are UK schemes for UK-based businesses. However, non-UK companies can also qualify if they set up a 'permanent establishment' in the UK, which means having a branch office with key members of staff here. This is more common than you might think. We work with a lot of French and Portuguese start-ups that want to raise investment in the UK. These countries have relatively low operating costs and a rich pool of skills and talent, but fewer tax-friendly investment schemes. So businesses there often open branches in the UK, which allow UK investors to invest in them and receive shares in the foreign company while still claiming tax relief from HMRC.

Your company must have the right structure

If you have a group structure, all tax-relief investment must be put into the top parent company. There are complex rules to determine what makes a parent company for these purposes, but a company that owns more than 50 percent of the issued shares will usually qualify.

Why might you want to insert a new parent company over a company that's already raised investment? The main reason would be if you want to make yourself more attractive to US investors by setting up a US holding company. This is a complicated area, but the main takeaway is that once you have EIS or SEIS in place, every decision relating to investments, shares, and restructuring should always be checked with your solicitor to avoid invalidating tax relief for your existing investors.

After you've gained investment

Some of the eligibility criteria for SEIS and EIS investment apply after you've gained investment, as well as at the time of it. However, there are other 'after the event' factors that you also need to understand if you're not to invalidate your eligibility. The main one is if you subsequently create the wrong kind of legal relationship between your investors and your business. You wouldn't do this on purpose, but it's surprisingly easy to do it by accident. The rules in this area are designed to prevent investors from artificially reducing their risk when investing under the schemes, and HMRC is diligent about applying them to the letter.

Investors can't be employees

I see this rule catching people out all the time. Investors who claim SEIS and EIS must be individuals – in other words, not investing under the umbrella of their companies. They also can't be an employee of the start-up, either at the time that they invest or for three years afterwards. It's not uncommon for the lead investor in a business to want to add value by working for it as an employee, and bam – there goes their SEIS or EIS tax relief. They'll have to repay it, and also shell out full tax on the gain they make when they sell their shares. The same applies if they become an executive director, although they can still be an advisory 'angel director' under SEIS rules.

An investor can, however, provide services to your company as a contractor or advisor. The amount you pay them has to be fair and reasonable compared to the market standard, and can't materially reduce the risk of their investment. This rule is designed to prevent investors from investing, then slowly clawing back their investment in the form of super-high fees, thereby reducing their risk. If you're thinking that you could get around this rule by paying your investor in shares or options instead, you're out of luck. If they're paid more in shares than their work is normally worth, it's the same situation. And if you pay them in options, HMRC will likely value them at the latest investment round price to when they were granted. This may have tax implications for your investor.

Investors can't hold shares already

At the time when they invest, an investor can't already hold shares in your start-up unless they're investment shares on which they've claimed tax relief through SEIS or EIS. This is another reason why your investors should be careful about taking share-based remuneration from you, as it could prevent them from investing again in your business in a tax-efficient way.

Investors can only hold certain types of shares

When investors invest, they must receive full risk ordinary shares with no protections or preferential rights, including extra voting rights. They also can't have security over assets, or anti-dilution protections. Basically they have to be treated the same as, or less well than, you and your co-founders. This is helpful, as it means that angels can't ask for unreasonable protections from you. As a final point, an investor investing under SEIS or EIS can't hold more than 30 percent of the shares, voting rights, or economic interest in your company.

Applying for advance assurance

Now that you know what you're not allowed to do, how do you check that you're eligible for SEIS or EIS investment in the first place? You apply for what's called 'advance assurance' from HMRC. This is what you show to your potential investors to prove that your company's trade qualifies for tax relief. HMRC usually takes four to six weeks to process your request, so ideally you should submit your application well before you start pitching.

If you meet the requirements, HMRC will send you a standard letter giving you the assurance. Brilliant, you think. But this letter isn't binding – it's only issued on the basis of the information that you've provided. The problem is that, in a well-meaning attempt to cut red tape and make the process simple, HMRC's advance assurance online form is deceptively easy to fill in.

I've seen situations in which founders have mistakenly entered information that was wrong, gained assurance, and once the investment has been completed and the money spent, had their investors' tax relief voided by HMRC. The investors have had to pay it back, often with charges and interest attached. Just as problematically, I've also seen entrepreneurs be refused assurance because they misunderstood their business model from a tax perspective, and so didn't describe it in the right way. Once HMRC has been told the wrong information and decided that a company doesn't qualify, it's difficult and expensive to persuade it to change its mind. It's essential to get things right from the start – claiming that you didn't have advice, and so didn't know what you were doing, doesn't really help.

One entrepreneur I met had set up a broker platform matching people who wanted credit with providers in a niche sector – think MoneySuperMarket.com but for a specific type of product. He applied for advance assurance, explaining that he was hoping to bring multiple credit providers to his platform to give his users the best possible choice. HMRC granted the assurance so he duly raised investment, issued the shares, and started building his platform.

But when it came to finalising the tax-relief position for his investors, he was stunned to be told that his company wasn't a qualifying business after all. Surely it must be a mistake – he'd been given advance assurance from the start. This is when he got in touch with us. It turned out that the entrepreneur had overlooked a tiny detail, which was that a broker platform (one that offers users multiple suppliers of credit) can qualify for SEIS and EIS, but one that provides only one option can't. Unfortunately for the founder, he'd not been able to bring on board as many providers as he'd hoped and had decided to work with one, yet he'd told HMRC that he'd have many. HMRC's advance assurance is based purely on what it's told, so if you don't give the whole story the assurance is worthless. Luckily we were able to resolve the issue, but it could have ended in tears.

If you're thinking of going through the process on your own and your business obviously falls within the rules, you may be fine – especially if you're only interested in SEIS investment. And here's a tip. In an attempt to filter out speculative applications, HMRC asks for details of your investors. However, it doesn't matter if those people don't end up investing. There's no reason to delay your application just because you don't have all your investors lined up and ready – just put down a couple of interested investors to be getting on with.

However, for an EIS round with its more complex rules and higher sums of money, I would advise against that approach. It's pretty much impossible to provide HMRC with everything it needs by completing the online form alone, and given that it isn't expensive to ask a solicitor or accountant to do the assurance for you, it makes sense to leave it to the experts. Whenever I submit applications I supply a thick pack of documents to HMRC, including the pitch deck or business plan. It's rare then for HMRC to come back later and query the company's eligibility. The last thing you want is to secure investment, spend the money, and find out that there's a problem.

What can you do after you've received investment?

I've already mentioned some actions that your company might take in the future that could retrospectively void your investors' eligibility for tax relief, such as employing an investor or paying them as an advisor at an inflated rate. However, there are others. SEIS and EIS are fiendishly complicated schemes with lots of intricate rules, and unfortunately it's easy to inadvertently break one of them by doing something that would never occur to you as being problematic. Here's a non-exhaustive list of the things that many businesses like yours do as a normal part of expanding, but which might invalidate your investors' tax-relief positions:

- carry out a share buyback;
- convert shares into different classes;
- put in place a liquidation preference on certain classes of share;
- put in place anti-dilution rights;
- insert a holding company above the company that raised the initial investment;
- buy another business;
- create a subsidiary that isn't wholly owned;
- make an investor an employee or executive director;
- re-domicile the start-up;
- make any preferential payments to an EIS investor;
- borrow money from an EIS investor; or
- issue any shares (other than for EIS investment) to an EIS investor.

What on earth are all these things, you may wonder? That's my point – you can't be expected to know, which is why you need to check before you make any structural or share-based changes to your company in the future. If the worst happens and you accidentally void your SEIS or EIS eligibility, your company will be barred from raising money from investors using the schemes ever again. That's not a great story to tell investors. Also, any investor who's bought into your company using the schemes in the previous three years may have to repay their upfront tax relief (plus interest and penalties), along with full capital gains tax on their sale proceeds when they come to sell their shares.

Getting the most from SEIS and EIS

These schemes are designed to help you to build your business, and they're one reason why the UK is such a brilliant place to be an entrepreneur. You should definitely be grabbing the opportunities they offer with both hands. However, given how complicated they are, and how much can go wrong, you also need to accept that this is an area in which tailored legal advice is invaluable.

The Treasury changes the rules every year in an attempt to shut down loopholes, often with a retrospective effect. For instance, a common way for investors to get around not being allowed to already hold shares in the company in which they want to invest is to ask for options instead. This works today, but I fully expect HMRC to block it in the future. If I was advising you I'd make sure that you and your investors were aware of this, because if the change happens, tax relief on any investments that your investors have made in the previous three years could be voided. That could land you in hot water.

Once you've raised investment attracting tax relief, it has long-term implications for everything that your business does. It's like getting married, buying a house, or moving abroad: one decision today can have a lifetime of implications. It's your – and your solicitor's – job to make sure that the long-term outcome is the one you want.

In the next chapter you'll discover the final steps to take to make your investment secure. You're almost at the finish point.

The wrap-up

- SEIS and EIS are tax-relief schemes that incentivise investors to buy into your start-up, and as such they're brilliant tools to help you grow your business.
- They also come with a fiendishly complex set of rules, which you should take legal advice on.
- Don't be lulled into a false sense of security by HMRC's simple form for gaining advance assurance – use a solicitor if you possibly can.

Chapter 11

Seal the deal

Receiving funds and issuing shares

Now that you know more about tax reliefs than you probably ever wanted to, I expect you're keen to understand the nuts and bolts of how the investment process works. How can you persuade investors to buy into your business? How do you strike a landmark deal that sets you up for the next year of growth? And how do you receive the money into your bank account and issue new shares? This is the moment you've been waiting for, when it all comes together in a big, beautiful reality.

To finalise the investment you'll sign documents that give your investors rights in respect of your company, and that sets the scene for how it will operate for the rest of its life. That means you need to understand the legal ins and outs of gaining funding, because while investment documentation for early stage investment isn't too complex, the ways in which the various documents fit together certainly is.

The process and documentation for investment

The process of raising investment usually follows a set pattern:

1. You prepare a pitch deck, business plan, and financial forecasts, making sure that they're optimised for both investors and HMRC.

2. You apply for advance assurance from HMRC, so you can prove to your investors that you're eligible for SEIS or EIS investment (we covered this in the last chapter).

3. You approach investors, pitch to them, and get them so excited about your business idea that they're keen to buy into your company.

4. You confirm that they're eligible to invest, which for UK angels usually means confirming that they're self-certified (more about this later).

5. Assuming that your investor wants to invest, your solicitor drafts a term sheet (which sets out the terms of the deal) for both parties to agree on.

6. Once you've negotiated the terms of the deal using the term sheet, your solicitor drafts the rest of the investment documentation. This will probably be made up of the subscription agreement, the share-holders' agreement, and the articles of association. The subscription agreement triggers the movement of money into your company and the issuing of shares. The shareholders' agreement is the document that regulates the relationship between investors and founders, describing how your business will be run and what rights your investors will have. And the articles of association set out the rules of your company now that you have investment, such as restrictions on share transfers and new share issues. In addition

to these documents, there are others such as board minutes and shareholder resolutions, in which the directors and shareholders authorise the investment round.

7. Your investor pays your start-up the money, and you issue shares to them.

8. You and your co-founders go out for a slap-up meal to celebrate.

Each of the documents I've mentioned plays an important role in you securing investment, so it's helpful to understand their roles. They also have critical tax and legal implications, which mean that the long-term viability of your company could be affected if you get them wrong.

The key pre-investment documents are as follows:

- pitch deck;
- business plan;
- cash flow and profit and loss forecasts; and
- term sheet.

Your pitch deck

This is a short series of eight to ten slides which should put across the key information about your business. Make it simple and informative, with any detailed analysis left to supporting documentation or your business plan. Investors see hundreds of pitch decks each year and don't have time to wade through reams of text, so keep yours brief. You can use it for a variety of purposes – to explain your idea to potential co-founders and advisors, to entice investors into investing, and to support an application to HMRC for advance assurance. Understanding the various audiences is important.

Introduction

Introduce the nature of your business, the sector it operates within, and the problem it's solving.

Explanation of your business

Describe what your start-up will do. What will it sell? How is it different to what else is in the marketplace? Give a sense of the size of the potential market and the share that you think it can achieve, showing your competitor research. By the end of this section your audience should be left in no doubt about what your business does (a surprising number of pitch decks don't achieve this).

Information about the founders and key employees

Investors want to know a little about the backgrounds and expertise of the founders and employees, so that they can feel confident that your team has the ability to deliver on its plans. Outline their experience, and share any household names that they may have worked for.

An explanation of your business strategy

How will you implement your idea and generate revenue? How profitable do you plan to be? What challenges do you foresee, and how will you overcome them? What are your key opportunities? Be upbeat but realistic with this – investors will quickly spot silly numbers.

Your marketing plan

Show that you've identified who your target customers are, and how you intend to recruit them. When will your marketing strategy kick in, and what are the metrics that will indicate success?

Financial forecasts

This part is crucial because both investors and HMRC want to know how you'll spend the investment money to deliver on your plans. They won't necessarily be looking for short-term profitability, but they will want to see that traction is possible and that there's a realistic prospect of long-term growth. Make sure that you can back up your numbers with a sound methodology – nothing puts off investors more than figures that seem to have been plucked from thin air. Also, make sure that you classify expenditure in the right way for HMRC, because simply using the wrong wording can be enough to result in your advance assurance being refused.

Exit plans

Although it's a long way away, investors will want to see that you've thought about when and how to exit. For most of them, this is the time when they'll gain their return on investment.

Overall, your pitch deck must look good. You're asking investors to part with a sizeable sum of money, so at the very least it should be branded, follow a coherent format, and be free from errors. Also, bear in mind that you won't necessarily be presenting it in person, for instance if you're emailing it to an angel investor who's expressed an interest. Some founders have two versions: one to talk through, and another slightly longer version that can stand on its own if needed.

Your business plan

It's tempting to see this as another piece of boring paperwork that you have to produce to secure funding. But your business plan isn't only for investors and HMRC. It's an important tool that helps you to clarify your thinking about your business, set your expectations, and hold yourself to account. If you copy one from elsewhere, or ask a 'business plan writer' to draft one for you, you're missing the point. You need to create the plan yourself, because otherwise you won't own the thinking behind it. Nor will you be able to defend it to investors or to HMRC (at least with any confidence). There's nothing wrong with asking someone who's a better wordsmith than you to write it up, but only if they base it on your ideas and calculations.

There's plenty of guidance out there already on how to create the perfect business plan, so I won't add to it here. However, what I will cover are the financial elements of your plan, because the way you present them will influence not only how successful you'll be in winning investment, but also whether you'll gain advance assurance from HMRC. If your investors are claiming tax relief you can inadvertently invalidate it by writing your business plan in the wrong way.

Your financial forecasts

Your cash flow and profit and loss forecasts are key elements of your business plan. They should cover the period during which the investment will be spent, and potentially some longer term forecasting up to three to five years after you gain investment.

Your cash flow forecast is the most important of the two, because it's the one that's likely to be most accurate at this stage. To generate it, you need to research what your costs should be. You can expect both HMRC and your potential investors to ask you to defend your financials, so if you've predicted that you can achieve a five percent market penetration within two years of launch, you should be able to show why. Statistics from your competitors, or your own beta testing, should support your numbers. Not backing up your figures with research is the number one reason for failing to impress investors, and it's often because people have outsourced the cash flow forecast to their accountant. Just like with your business plan, it's fine to have help with making sense of the figures and presenting them, but you need to understand them.

I'm amazed that anyone can aim to raise money, and yet not know how much they need or why. For instance, one entrepreneur I spoke to had allocated £1,500 for legal fees for the first two years of his start-up. He'd assumed that he wouldn't need any solicitors to help him raise a £1 million seed round from a mixed group of angels and VCs, and he also hadn't realised that his business was carrying out regulated activities. It's important to base your forecasts on sensible assumptions, and it may be that you need expert help to judge what a sensible assumption is.

Make sure your business plan is HMRC-friendly

This is where your business plan links to the tax relief that your investors will probably be claiming. When you apply for advance assurance from HMRC, you have to show how your investment money will be spent. If you've thought through your business plan properly, you'll have the information at your fingertips. If you haven't, you might give them the wrong forecasts because you'll be guessing.

For instance, one of HMRC's requirements is that the expenditure of EIS investment money should lead to the organic growth of employees, revenue, and customer numbers. If you tell HMRC that three months after receiving investment you'll employ an office manager at £30,000 a year, and two months later a developer at £60,000 a year, HMRC will be impressed that you're increasing your number of employees. But if it was just a nice story you made up to impress the tax man, and you end up spending all the money on failed social media ads instead, HMRC can retrospectively void your investors' tax reliefs. You've not achieved organic growth in any of the three key areas, and have done entirely different things with the money to what you told HMRC.

Everything to do with raising investment hinges on your business plan. It makes you think about what you'll do, and it gives you accurate information to pass to investors and HMRC. It's crucial to think it through using your own ideas, research, and numbers.

Your term sheet

This is the first document that you'll draw up after you've 'warmed up' your investors. A term sheet isn't legally binding, so some founders assume that it's okay to write their own or copy someone else's. That's a mistake, because your term sheet sets out the crucial commercial terms between you and your investors. If you decide later on that you've got the terms wrong, you'll find that your investors will be highly resistant to re-visiting them. They're busy people who tend to make their decisions once.

Angels usually prefer you to create your own term sheet, but VCs almost always have their own. If you're working with an angel investor you should ideally ask your solicitor to draft it, and if it's already been drawn up by a VC fund, ask them to review it. Any solicitor who works in the start-up space should be able to carry out a quick review, maybe even for free if they're hopeful of winning further business from you.

As well as your term sheet, there's a raft of other documentation which needs to be negotiated and signed. However, it's important that you create it *after* your investors have agreed to the term sheet. If there are points that investors want to discuss, it's much easier to do it based on a two-page list of terms than a full suite of investment documents. If you give them the long-form documentation too soon, you risk them getting bogged down in detail and not making a decision, or pushing back on all manner of points that would otherwise not have been an issue. Think of it from their point of view. They haven't made the final decision to invest in your business yet, and the first thing they receive is a stack of paperwork. They feel obliged to review it, which leads them to draw the wrong conclusions from some of the more unfamiliar clauses, and they assume that you're trying to be aggressive and unreasonable. Often the result is that they back out.

As evidence for this, out of the 850 investment rounds that my firm has worked on in the past decade, we've lost only nine. Five of them were due to the investment deep freeze after the Brexit referendum, and four were because the founders insisted on providing the long-form documentation instead of a two-page term sheet. The investors pulled out because the deal seemed too complicated for them – it wasn't. In my experience, once the term sheet is agreed it's rare for the other documentation to cause a major problem, and you may even find that your investment money is paid before it's all signed. Happy days!

How detailed should your term sheet be? This is where the Goldilocks principle comes in. The point of the term sheet is to help your investors to understand the terms of the deal so that they can make a decision. If it's too simple, they'll save their decision making for when they see the long-form documentation (which you don't want). If it's too long, you'll risk having a drawn-out negotiation in which everyone argues about the details. The optimal length is a couple of pages, with a paragraph on each of the main terms in layperson's language.

Here are some tips for creating your term sheet, and an explanation of what the key clauses mean.

Current share capital

Investors want to see a breakdown of your existing share capital on the term sheet, because their investment calculations are based on this information. It sounds obvious, but make sure you know who your current shareholders are, and that the shares they hold match your records at Companies House (you may have never got around to issuing shares to your co-founders, for instance). There's no need to delay your round because of this, as you can issue outstanding shares in parallel with the negotiations. You do need to be aware of it, though.

Valuations

Include the pre-money valuation, the total amount that you're trying to raise, and the percentage of shares in your company that your investors will receive based on the amount of investment. Remember to calculate the investor percentage using the *post-money* valuation (see Chapter 8 for why). Including these figures prevents your investors from getting the maths wrong later, which happens more often than you might think. Don't include a detailed post-investment cap table because it will only cause confusion, especially if the investment amounts change before you finalise the deal. And there's no need to list all the potential investors individually as these may also change. Keep things simple.

Timeline

Setting a timeline for the completion of the round helps to manage expectations. If you don't add one in, your investors will make up their own timings and things can get messy.

Exclusivity

Some VCs ask for exclusivity, in which you agree not to raise money from anyone else for a certain period of time. My view is that you should avoid this where possible, because you don't want to be tied to an investor whom you might not want to work with later.

Directorships

There are two sources of power within your company: directors, who run the day-to-day business and make up the board, and shareholders, who are consulted on more important matters. You and your co-founders should hold the majority of directorships, giving you a majority vote on board decisions.

In your early rounds you won't want to give your investors a board seat, nor do you need to. However, with more experienced investors, you might want to give them a board observer right. This is the right to attend board meetings and contribute to the discussions but without having a vote, and can be a way of keeping your investors engaged without you giving away control.

Fees and costs

You shouldn't pay any fees to angel investors, nor should you pay their legal costs. Some VC funds impose fees, and if they're excessively high you should negotiate them down.

Information rights

Some founders are reluctant to send company performance information to their investors, for fear of it triggering a monthly hour-long phone call in which they have to give a blow-by-blow account of their decisions. I have to say, this approach bugs me. Your early stage investors take a lot of risk and yet they have minimal rights, especially compared to VCs in later rounds. The one right they do have is to receive information, which should include a summary financial analysis, performance against key performance indicators (KPIs), and annual statutory accounts. Given that you have to produce most of this anyway, I can't see what's wrong with passing it to your angels so they can discuss it with you if they want to. In my experience, founders who hold their cards too close to their chest go on to have poor relationships with their investors, which means that if they need their support in the future it's in short supply.

Share issue and transfer restrictions

There are various technical clauses relating to how shares are issued and transferred. In short, they're as follows.

Pre-emption on transfer

Under this provision, if any shareholder wants to sell their shares and has a buyer lined up, they must first offer the shares to the existing shareholders at the same price and terms as offered by the potential buyer. This allows your existing shareholders (which includes you, possibly your co-founders, and other investors) to stop a new person coming in, by buying the shares offered for sale.

Drag-along

When you and your co-founders come to sell your company, you don't want a minority shareholder to block the deal by refusing to sell their shares. This provision prevents that from happening. As long as your buyer secures the right to buy more than a specified percentage of your company's shares (often 50 percent), they can force the other shareholders to sell their shares to them at the same price and terms. There are lots of variations on this clause, which depend on the stage of your business and who your investors are.

Tag-along

This is the flip side of a drag-along, and is more of a protection for your investors than it is for you and your co-founders. It's most relevant when you and your co-founders want to exit. If a potential buyer of your company manages to secure the right to purchase more than a specified percentage of your company's shares, they must make an offer to all the other shareholders (which they don't have to accept) to buy their shares at the same price and terms. This means that minority shareholders won't be left stranded when you exit.

Pre-emption on allotment

This provision enables your investors to avoid their shareholding percentage being diluted. If you want to issue any further shares (perhaps as part of a future investment round), you must first offer them to your existing shareholders at the same price and terms as you're offering to new investors. This allows your existing shareholders to invest their pro-rata percentage of the new round to ensure that they're not diluted.

For instance, imagine that one of your investors holds ten percent of your company. You want to issue further shares to a new investor, who will pay in £100,000. With their pre-emption rights, your existing investor can buy ten percent of that round if they want to. Their percentage of the company therefore remains at an undiluted ten percent (although they have to invest more to keep it there).

It's important to carve out certain types of share issue from these provisions. This might include, for instance, an exercise of options, to ensure that you're able to allow your option holders to exercise their options without shareholders taking up their pre-emption rights.

Consent rights

When you make important business decisions, by default certain matters need to be approved by a specific percentage of your shareholders – either 50 or 75 percent, depending on the decision itself. However, your investors are minority shareholders, which means that (depending on what percentage you and your co-founders hold in total) you and your co-founders are effectively free to do what you want. It's therefore quite common (and not a bad idea) to set out a short list of activities that need the consent of a majority of investors. These include things like you and your co-founders paying yourselves over a certain amount, the company granting security over its assets, or the business being wound up. Not offering any consent rights in your term sheet will probably result in your investors proposing their own three-page list, so it's best to pre-empt them with your own, shorter one.

Warranties

How do your investors know that what you've told them is true? For instance, you could have claimed that your company owns all of its IP but have made a mistake or deliberately misled them. The way that investors protect themselves against this is by asking your company (or you personally) to give warranties. These are contractual promises that certain statements are true at the split second that the investment round is closed. If they ask you for a warranty that isn't true, you have to explain why in a letter that goes along with the transaction documentation. If you don't come clean, you may have to compensate your investors later (subject to any limitations that your solicitor has cleverly included).

Be warned that warranties can trip you up, because they often cover circumstances that are obvious to solicitors and not to you. You'd have to be brave or stupid to agree to any substantive list of warranties without your solicitor reviewing them. I've often been told by entrepreneurs that, 'Oh, the warranties are fine, we don't need to disclose anything.' I've then run through them in detail, and ended up with pages of disclosures. You should also be aware that if you (rather than your company) give warranties, you're personally liable if they turn out to be untrue and you haven't disclosed the reasons why. If you have to pay compensation to your investors for breaking your warranties, it can also break your bank balance.

As with investor consent rights, it's best to give a limited list of innocuous warranties rather than to exclude them altogether. Investors who are familiar with investment documentation will expect to see some, and the last thing you want is for them to produce their own, multi-page list.

Other provisions

There are some other, more complicated provisions which may appear in a term sheet for a later investment round, so I won't go into them here. They cover such exciting topics as liquidation preference, anti-dilution provision, ratchets, and co-sale rights. I'll say it again: get legal advice on the impact of these. If you're not careful they can invalidate your investors' entitlement to SEIS and EIS, reduce the chances of your early stage investors achieving an exit, and have numerous other unintended consequences.

The term sheet summarises the key terms of the long-form documentation. Once it's agreed, your solicitor will start drafting the subscription agreements, shareholders' agreement, and amended articles. With luck you can close your round in two to four weeks!

Receiving your money and issuing shares

You've pitched your idea, you've written your business plan, you've agreed your term sheet, and all the necessary documentation has been signed. Now comes the moment you've been waiting for: the arrival of a big, fat set of zeros in your company bank account.

But first, there are some things that you need to know about the process of receiving your investment and issuing shares. If you get them wrong – and many do – you can (you guessed it) invalidate your investors' rights to claim SEIS and EIS. You might think that your investors would be clued up enough about the rules to sort this out for themselves, but often they aren't. They expect you to know what to do. HMRC can be flexible with some aspects of SEIS and EIS, but this is one area in which they won't co-operate if you make a mistake.

The issues hinge on two key provisions of SEIS and EIS:

- You have to receive *all* of your investment money from a specific investor *before* you issue shares to them. I suggest leaving one business day between receiving funds and issuing shares, so that there's no doubt in the matter.
- This is specific to SEIS. Your company's net asset value must be below £200,000 *at the point when you issue SEIS shares to investors*.

Let's say that you're raising a £600,000 investment round. If you have to receive the money before you issue the SEIS shares, your company could well have a net asset value of more than £200,000 before the shares are issued, due to the investors' cash in the company's bank account. It's a catch-22 situation. However, the way you get around it is to have all the investment money paid into your solicitor's bank account rather than your company one. Your solicitor will transfer the SEIS money to you and issue the SEIS shares, and then issue the balance of money to you and issue shares for that.

On another note, the situation is complicated by the fact that you'll probably be raising a round made up of both SEIS and EIS investment, and by law SEIS shares must be issued at least a day before EIS shares.

If this sounds difficult to manage, it's not – the timings in the following list will help you to work out what to do when. I'm using the example of a mixed round of £600,000 investment, made up of £250,000 SEIS, £200,000 EIS, and £150,000 non-tax-relief money.

Business day 1: SEIS monies of £250,000 paid by your solicitor into your company bank account.

Business day 2: you issue SEIS shares.

Business day 3: EIS monies of £200,000 paid by your solicitor into your company bank account.

Business day 4: you issue EIS shares.

Business day 5: non-tax-relief monies of £150,000 paid directly into your company bank account.

Business day 6: you issue non-tax-relief shares.

After you've issued all of the shares, you (or your solicitor) will complete a form to claim the tax relief for your investors and send it to HMRC. There's one form for SEIS and another for EIS, called SEIS1 and EIS1 respectively. You have to complete a separate form for each day on which you issue shares, and HMRC takes around four weeks to review them. It will then send you an authorisation (an SEIS2 or EIS2), which allows you to issue another form (SEIS3 or EIS3) to each investor. These can be downloaded online, with you filling in one page and your investor another. Never – repeat, never – be tempted to complete a form 3 until you've received authority from HMRC. It's a criminal offence. And if this is clear as mud to you, ask your solicitor or accountant to do it for you.

As well as this, your solicitor will make a variety of filings with Companies House and update your company's shareholder register.

The financial promotions regime

Somewhere in the fundraising process you need to make sure that you've complied with what's called the 'financial promotions regime'. This is a law that protects people from making high-risk investments without taking financial advice. According to the regime, it's illegal to make 'an invitation or inducement to engage in investment activity, communicated by a person in the course of business', unless:

- the person making the financial promotion is authorised by the Financial Conduct Authority (FCA);

- the content of the communication has been approved by an authorised person in accordance with the FCA rules; or
- the communication is covered by an exemption.

The provision of a term sheet is definitely considered to be an invitation to engage in investment activity, as may also be the sending of a pitch deck, depending on the content. Given that you won't have authorisation from the FCA to make a financial promotion, and your term sheet is unlikely to have been approved by an authorised person, you'll need to rely on your investor falling within one of the exempted categories. The purpose of the exemptions is to ensure that the people you're asking to invest in your business have enough financial know-how to make sensible decisions. These are the exemptions most relevant to you:

- **Certified high-net-worth individuals.** This is the most common one. These are people who earn, or have assets, over a certain threshold. You should ask them to sign a certificate to prove this, which your solicitor can give you standard wording for.
- **Self-certified sophisticated investors.** These are people who meet one of a number of conditions. They could be members of networks, or syndicates of business angels. They could be people who've made more than one investment in an unlisted company in the previous two years. They could be working as professionals in the private equity sector, or in the provision of finance for small and medium enterprises.

Or they could be directors of companies with annual turnovers of at least £1 million. Just as with a certified high-net-worth individual certificate, your solicitor can give you a statement for a self-certified sophisticated investor.

Do all start-ups bother with complying with the financial promotions regime? I'll admit, many don't. But the rules on financial promotions are designed to cover a wide variety of activities and come with a nasty sting in the tail, as if you breach the regime you'll have committed a criminal offence. You could also be held personally liable for any investors' losses in your business. Given that getting it right is easy, it's worth building it into your fundraising process, even if you only do it when you complete the round. Whenever we manage an investment round we ask each investor to sign an exemption form, either when the term sheet goes out or when the transaction documents are signed. The forms sit in the company's compliance file, and everyone sleeps at night.

This relates to one of my key themes in these chapters about tax relief and investment. Many entrepreneurs see investment documentation as a necessary evil – as something to spend as little as possible on, like car insurance. So they treat it as a commodity and buy it off the shelf, or they lift it from what someone else has used (or an investor has given them) and reckon that will probably do. This approach doesn't make sense. If you want a nice relaxing read in the bath, you don't just grab the first book you find – it could end up being one you hate even if a friend told you it was a page-turner. Instead, you pick a book that's right for you. Legal documentation is the same: two documents with the title 'shareholders' agreement' can contain completely different provisions. One might give your investors far too much control, and one might be just what you need.

For this crucial transaction in your company's life you need documentation that's tailored to your business objectives, your approach to managing your team and investors, and your own needs. Your entrepreneur buddy might assure you that her contract is 'pretty market standard' so you can copy it for yourself, but I've heard this countless times. Every time I've looked through 'standard' documents, I've seen onerous terms that are anything but standard, and that would be damaging to the business intending to use them. Your start-up is different from – and better than – everyone else's, so why use the same documents? Get tailored advice, get it early, and get it from a proper solicitor. Their responsibility is to make the complicated simple so that you don't have to figure it all out for yourself. Then you can get on with your proper (and much more enjoyable) job, which is expanding your business using the fabulous investment money you've gained.

The wrap-up

- Raising investment involves generating key pieces of documentation that not only influence whether you receive the money in the first place, but also whether you inadvertently lose it in the future.
- These documents can also dictate the future direction of your company, and whether or not you can expand in years to come.

- Working with an experienced solicitor means that you'll not make mistakes that could cost you later, as well as open up more opportunities for you.

How's Lucio doing?

We left Lucio feeling relieved and ecstatic that he's now lined up some interested investors. He knows that his next step is to apply for advance assurance from HMRC, but he hasn't realised that it'll take four to six weeks to come back. This sends him into a panic. He scrambles around to see if his investors will invest without it, but they won't. Kicking himself for not knowing about the delay, and seeing that the application form is nice and straightforward, he considers doing it himself. Luckily, while talking to his solicitor about something else, he learns that the DIY approach for a mixed round of £1.5 million of SEIS and EIS money isn't a good idea. This is backed up by the last of his investors, who's putting in the final £200,000: 'I'm investing on the basis of tax relief,' he says. 'There's no way I'm going ahead if you've done the advance assurance yourself.'

So Lucio has it carried out properly by his solicitor, who also points out that his cash flow forecast is way off beam. It shows £50 million profit in three years, which is far too optimistic. The solicitor explains that not only will HMRC think there's not enough risk in the business, but also that he'll lose credibility and his investors may walk away. So he re-creates his forecast and has a chat to his investors about it, who are fine with the more reasonable estimates.

Lucio's final issue is IP. His company owns the IP in the Pre-Train platform, but his clients will own the IP for the training materials they load onto it. One of his investors tells Lucio that this makes him ineligible for SEIS or EIS investment, because not all of the IP on his platform has been created by his business. This sends Lucio into another panic, but after a chat with his solicitor he learns that this isn't the case. The IP that generates Pre-Train's revenue is the IP of the platform, not that of his client's content. Given that what he's selling to investors is the platform, he's okay. It's lucky that he checked it out.

Solid foundations

You've learned a heap of truths about business law – facts you wanted to know, facts you didn't want to know, and in many cases facts you had no idea you didn't know about. Possessing this information makes the difference between your start-up being built on sand and it being built on rock. With sand, the ground is never solid beneath your feet – you could find yourself being sued or missing out on a key opportunity, all because of something that you didn't expect to be a problem. With rock, you're secure – you know you have your main risks covered, and you're free to go all out with your business-building.

Taken as a whole, the concepts that you've learned might feel a bit overwhelming. I suggest actioning them step by step, or chapter by chapter. Don't forget that on page 213 is a start-up checklist that will help you to break down your tasks into ten manageable stages, so feel free to refer to that.

You might also find it helpful to consider the four start-up themes that have emerged throughout the book:

- talking about your business idea, rather than being secretive about it;
- knowing when to be a commercial realist, and when to be a perfectionist;
- the importance of identifying and managing your risks; and
- understanding when to ask for bespoke advice, and when to do things yourself.

Talking about your business idea

There's nothing to lose, and everything to gain, by talking to as many people as possible about your business idea before you start making it a reality. This will help you to finesse it according to what people actually want, rather than to what you think would work. You'll also increase your chances of stumbling across a chance investor who might fall in love with it, or a useful contact who can point you in the direction of a top class web developer or social media specialist. People love to help and advise, so it doesn't make sense to keep your cards close to your chest.

If you're worried that someone will steal your idea, believe me – it's generally not something to worry about. That's because building a successful business is as much about your passion and expertise as it is about the core idea it's based on. From my experience of working with countless start-ups, I've learned that it's almost impossible to predict whether or not a business concept will be successful. I've concluded that it's execution that's key, and that's down to you.

Commercial realism versus perfectionism

Good entrepreneurs learn to judge when to be a perfectionist and when to be a realist. The vast majority of the time, realism is the way to go. Spending your time poring over details, especially ones that you don't fully understand, saps your time and energy and kills your innovative spirit. You have specific skills to bring to your start-up, and you'll do best if you embrace your strengths.

However, there are also moments when you need to pay attention to the details – especially if they're legal and financial ones. This is when finding support to fill in the gaps comes in, as it's an important way to compensate for the areas in which you're lacking knowledge and understanding. My point here is that it's not you who has to be the perfectionist, but the experts whom you choose to help you. Your solicitor, accountant, and software developer, for instance, have a responsibility to get their details right. Your role is to learn enough about these subjects so that you can spot where the main problems might lurk, and then to use their guidance to help you solve them.

Identifying and managing your risks

Essentially, running a successful business comes down to knowing which risks to take and which to avoid. If a risk is low, you can live with it. But if it's high, you need help in removing or reducing it. When companies go bust or lose vast sums of money, it's usually because they didn't spot the risks coming over the horizon. And yet risk management doesn't have to be a scary or complicated area – it just requires sensible and tailored advice.

Imagine that a friend bets you that you'd never have the guts to organise your own bungee jump. If you have any sense you'll politely decline the offer, but let's say that you rashly decide to accept. What's your first task? It's to source a strong rope, a harness, and the mechanism that secures everything to the bridge you're going to jump off. Would you buy some standard cord from your local DIY store? Of course not – it wouldn't be right for the job. It wouldn't be elastic and would snap under your weight. Instead, you go to a specialist store that sells ropes for bungee jumps. You take advice from the manager, and plump for a mid-range rope that's suitable for your purpose – one bungee jump.

When it comes to doing the jump, do you trundle up to the bridge and figure out how to set up the equipment yourself? Again, probably not. You find someone who knows about bungee jumping and ask them to assemble everything for you. This is the equivalent of asking for expert advice in setting up your business – something that will be your life and livelihood for many years to come, and may deliver millions when you come to sell it. You wouldn't hurl yourself off a bridge attached to a basic rope, so why would you throw yourself into a start-up with the legal equivalent?

Equally, your start-up doesn't need a solicitor who works with Apple or Google and charges £1,000 an hour. That's the equivalent of buying a bungee rope that contains golden thread so it sparkles in the sun – it's not necessary and might not even give you the results you need. Instead, you want an expert who can reduce your risks by giving you the right level of input. And a suitable rope.

Bespoke advice versus the DIY approach

If the past ten years of advising new businesses on their legal and commercial risks have taught me anything, it's that each start-up is different and therefore has its own needs. One of the biggest mistakes that entrepreneurs make is to view legal support in a commoditised way, buying solutions off the shelf or trying to do everything themselves. This exposes them to legal problems, and in the worst cases can shut down lucrative deals that would have been theirs for the taking. Your start-up is special, so you need to treat it that way.

Then, when you've dealt with the main threats to your success, you're freed up to focus on the more exciting aspects of your start-up – the areas you're good at, and that will bring you the rewards. Knowing that you're unlikely to have to fight a costly lawsuit, or spend hours of your time arguing with customers or investors with unrealistic expectations, is enormously freeing. After all, you didn't create your start-up so that you could spend sleepless nights worrying about whether you've messed up your investment documentation, but so that you could sell shed-loads of products or services to thousands of customers and build an amazing brand.

Goodbye Lucio

When we first met Lucio he was sitting in a London cafe, contemplating his idea for an online business matching corporates with potential job applicants. He's come a long way since then. His platform is up and running, he's signed his first major client, and he's built relationships with a range of business experts on whom he can call when he needs advice. This has given him a sound understanding of his risks.

Today, as a marker of his progress, he's taking a nostalgic return trip to that same cafe. Stirring his cappuccino and scrolling through his phone contacts, he can't resist a smile. Investors, advisors, co-founders – they're all in there. One contact is his solicitor, who he now has on speed dial. Every time he has a significant decision to make, such as whether to change the way he charges for his services or to seek more investment, he picks up the phone. Usually it's only a five-minute conversation, but it helps him to relax when he hears that he's not about to do something that could invalidate his investor tax relief or cause other problems. This has given him the confidence to throw himself into developing and marketing his site. Pre-Train is going full steam ahead.

Lucio's business has solid foundations – it's built on rock. And now, yours is too. Good luck!

Start-up checklist

There are many things to think about when you start a business, so I've created this handy checklist to help you tick off the tasks. Apart from the first item it's not necessarily in priority order, as that will depend on your circumstances. Beside each task is the name of the chapter that talks you through what to do.

1. Incorporate your company – *Chapter 1*
2. Buy the right insurance – *Chapter 2*
3. Check for competing business names – *Chapter 3*
4. Make everyone sign a transfer of IP document – *Chapter 3*
5. Ask a solicitor to draw up your customer contract – *Chapter 5*
6. Carry out a data protection review – *Chapter 6*
7. Decide what kind of funding you need to expand – *Chapter 7*
8. Value your company – *Chapter 8*
9. Find out if your business qualifies for investor tax reliefs and apply for advance assurance – *Chapter 10*
10. Pitch to investors and secure funding – *Chapter 11*

All readers of this book are entitled to a free consultation with Michael or one of his colleagues at Buckworths. Just email office@buckworths.com and quote code 'BOR2'.

The author

Michael Buckworth is the founder of Buckworths, the only law firm in the UK working exclusively with start-ups and high-growth businesses. With offices in London and Manchester, most of the firm's clients are technology businesses, with half of them in the fin-tech space. The remainder are an intriguing mix of product companies, restaurants, and advisory firms.

Michael has a passion for entrepreneurialism, and in the ten years that Buckworths has been in existence, has advised over 1,200 start-ups. His conviction is that every new business is different and deserves advice that's tailored to its specific risks. Experience has shown him that one of the biggest mistakes entrepreneurs make is to view legal services as commoditised. This approach exposes them to potential pitfalls, and can deny them valuable opportunities.

Originally Michael studied law at Oxford University. He then spent several years at the London offices of two of the world's top-ranked New York law firms, Shearman & Sterling LLP and Cleary Gottlieb Steen & Hamilton LLP. He's been 'entrepreneur in residence' at London South Bank University and University College, London, for several years, and works closely with City University's entrepreneur scheme. Michael speaks regularly at industry events, and enjoys lobbying government around the subject of start-ups.

If you'd like to ask Michael for legal advice, or to speak at one of your events, please contact him at office@buckworths.com or on 020 7952 1723. You can see his firm's website at www.buckworths.com.

Acknowledgements

I'd been talking about writing a book for over five years, and never quite got around to it. The COVID-19 pandemic provided me with an opportunity to get it done, and I'm so glad that I did. I must give a huge thank you to Ginny Carter for wading through pages of technical legal concepts and random opinions, and creating something intelligible and easy to read. Her own book, *Your Business Your Book*, is a must for anyone thinking of writing a book. It certainly helped me enormously with this one.

Neither this book nor my firm would exist without the work of Ivan Gerovski, my COO at Buckworths. It hasn't always been easy, but we manage to keep the plates spinning year after year. Ivan, I don't thank you enough for what you do, so here's some appreciation from me in print.

To Davide and Tobes, thanks for tolerating the repeated weekends of research and writing. Your humour and support were invaluable.

I can't leave out my family, who thought I was mad to quit City law and set up my own firm. Despite your concerns, you've always been supportive and listened to my repeated streams of consciousness. Your role of unofficial counsellor has helped to keep me (relatively) sane. I love you all very much.

Last and by no means least, thank you to all of my clients who've supported me and Buckworths over the years. Some of you have been with us from the beginning, and your loyalty is massively appreciated.